INSECTS

Illustrations by
Gordon Riley

text by
Michael Chinery

COLLINS
London and Glasgow

First published 1986
© in the text Michael Chinery 1986
© in the illustrations Gordon Riley 1986
ISBN 0 00 458818 5
Colour reproduction by Adroit Photo-Litho Ltd, Birmingham
Filmset by Wordsmiths Typesetting, London
Printed and bound by Wm Collins Sons and Co Ltd, Glasgow
Reprint 10 9 8 7 6 5 4 3 2 1 0

Contents

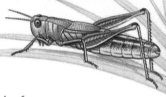

How to use this book

This book is designed to help you to name some of the common insects and other 'creepie-crawlies' that you find around you, and to tell you something of their habits – why they live in your garden, for example, and what they do there. There is a short introductory text for each major group, which should be read in conjunction with the individual descriptions. Technical terms have been avoided except for an unavoidable few, explained in the book's introduction. We include some of the commonest and most conspicuous species from Europe's 100,000 insects. If you find something that is not *quite* like one of the pictures it is probably a close relative.

Size Insects are shown at natural size, or, where this is not so, magnification or reduction is given alongside. Individuals can vary a great deal in size. Plants are not shown to scale.

Sex Unless otherwise stated, in the introduction to each group or in the individual descriptions, the sexes are more or less alike. Where they differ significantly the male is indicated by ♂ and the female by ♀.

Range Unless otherwise stated, the insects can be found in suitable habitats throughout western Europe. For the purposes of this book, northern Europe means Scandinavia and Finland; central Europe extends from Denmark and the British Isles to a line joining Bordeaux and Venice; and southern Europe is everything to the south of this line.

Introduction

Roughly a million different kinds of insects have been discovered and named up to now – far more than all the other kinds of animals put together. Nearly 100,000 live in Europe, and about 20,000 of these live in the British Isles. Hundreds of new species are being discovered every year, especially in tropical areas. Very few insects live in the sea, but they have managed to conquer virtually everywhere else and, between them, they eat almost everything – from nectar to blood and from solid wood to rotting dung. This adaptability is one reason why the insects are such a successful group of animals.

Insects belong with the crabs, spiders and a few other creatures in the huge group of animals known as arthropods. This name literally means 'jointed feet', and if you look closely at the legs of any of these animals you will see that they all consist of a number of distinct segments separated from each other by flexible joints. Adult insects have three pairs of these jointed legs - less than the other arthropods – and only the insects have wings.

The insect body

An insect is encased in a tough coat with flexible joints that enable it to move. This coat, which is rather like a suit of armour, is the arthropod version of a skeleton. The body has three main regions, known as the head, thorax and abdomen. Although the wings sometimes conceal the junction between the thorax and the abdomen, the three regions are sharply separated, often with such a narrow neck or waist between them that the insect looks almost as if it has been sawn apart. This is why insects are so called: the name literally means 'cut into'.

The head carries a pair of feelers or antennae, which help the insect to find its way about. They carry hundreds of minute sense organs which can detect scent, sound, air currents and even heat. They help the insect to locate food and mates and also to detect approaching enemies. There are two fairly large eyes in most insects, known as compound eyes because each is composed of several or many separate lenses. Dragonflies, which spot and capture prey in mid-air, have thousands of lenses in each eye, and the eyes occupy almost all of the head. Many insects also have some simpler eyes known as ocelli. There are usually three, forming a triangle on the top of the head, but they cannot form images and probably do no more than detect light and dark.

Three types of insect antennae.

Insects have no internal jaws, or any other internal skeleton, and they feed with the aid of a number of much modified limbs, known as mouth-parts. These surround the mouth and vary enormously with the diets of the insects. There are, however, two main types: biting mouth-parts, for dealing with solid food, and sucking mouth-parts, for taking in liquids. Biting mouth-parts, which cut and chew the food before shoving it into the mouth, are best seen among the wasps, beetles and grasshoppers. Sucking mouth-parts are found in the bugs and flies, and also in the butterflies and moths. Those of the bugs and the blood-sucking flies are like miniature hypodermic needles (*see page 64*) and are used to pierce plants or animals to get at their juices. The mouth-parts are very often equipped with sensory branches, known as palps, which help to detect food and also taste it to make sure that it is suitable before the insect starts to feed.

The thorax carries the wings, when they are present, and the three pairs of legs. Most adult insects have two pairs of wings, although the true flies (*see page 106*) have only one pair. The wings are normally membranous and supported by a network of veins, whose arrangement is often of great importance in classifying the insects. Beetles have greatly modified forewings which are tough and horny and which normally cover almost all of the body, including the flimsy hind wings. Earwigs, grasshoppers, and most bugs have similarly toughened and protective fore-wings. But not all insects have wings. The bristletails

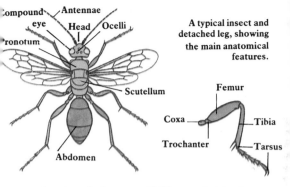

A typical insect and detached leg, showing the main anatomical features.

Labels on the insect: Compound eye, Antennae, Head, Ocelli, Pronotum, Scutellum, Abdomen

Labels on the leg: Femur, Coxa, Trochanter, Tibia, Tarsus

and springtails (*see pages 18-19*) are primitive insects that have never had wings at any time in their history. Fleas and lice and some other parasites are also wingless, although they had winged ancestors. They gradually lost their wings during their evolution, for what is the point of wings when you live deep down in the fur or feathers of your host? Even among groups that are normally fully-winged there are some wingless species or species with much reduced wings. In young insects the wings are never fully developed.

The thorax is covered by a number of tough plates – all part of the outer skeleton. The front one is known as the pronotum. It is little more than a narrow collar in many insects, but in grasshoppers, bugs and beetles it is very large – often covering much of the head as well as the bulk of the thorax. Towards the rear of the thorax there is often a roughly triangular plate known as the scutellum. It is particularly noticeable in bugs, forming a prominent triangle between the bases of the forewings and sometimes extending back over much of the abdomen.

The legs vary a good deal in shape, according to the insects' habits, but all are built on the same plan – best seen in a large beetle or a grasshopper. The basal segment, which hinges on the thorax, is the coxa. It is usually quite small and is followed by an even smaller segment known as the trochanter. This is rigidly attached to the femur, and often difficult to pick out, but it plays no part in the identification of the insects in this book. The femur is usually the largest segment of the leg, although not necessarily the longest. It is followed by the tibia, which is generally long and slender. The leg ends with the foot or tarsus, which consists of between one and five small segments and usually has one or two small claws at the tip. You can see from the illustrations here and throughout the book how the proportions of the leg segments vary from one type of insect to another, and how they are modified for different tasks.

The legs also bear various sense organs, including hairs and bristles that are sensitive to touch and to air currents. Organs of smell and taste are generally concentrated on the tarsi, so that many insects taste their food merely by landing on it! Crickets even have their ears on their front legs, at the top of each tibia just below the 'knee'.

The abdomen has no legs in the adult insect, although it may carry a number of appendages at the hind end. These include the thread-like 'tails' of the bristletails and mayflies and the pincers of the earwigs. Several groups also have prominent mating and egg-laying equipment at the rear end. Many male bush crickets and dragonflies have conspicuous claspers with which they hold the females during mating. Female bush crickets have swordlike egg-layers, known as ovipositors, with which they poke their eggs into the soil or into slits in plants. Many ichneumons and other parasites (*see pages 144-5*) have prominent needle-like ovipositors which they use to pierce their victims and inject their eggs.

Insect life histories

Nearly all insects begin life as eggs, although the aphids and a few other insects may bring forth active young. The youngsters have no wings and most have to undergo considerable change, known as metamorphosis, before becoming adults. The exceptions are the bristletails and other primitive wingless insects (*see pages 18-19*), in which the youngsters resemble the adults in all but size and grow up with virtually no change in their appearance.

The insect's outer casing does not grow with the body and so, every time it gets too tight, the insect, like the other arthropods, has to stop growing to change its skin. There may be up to 50 of these changes, or moults, in an insect's lifetime, although most species moult between four and ten times. With the exception of the bristletails and springtails the insects stop moulting once they reach maturity.

The winged insects can be divided into two major groups according to the way in which their wings develop. In one group they develop gradually on the outside of the body, getting larger at each moult and becoming functional at the final moult, when the insect becomes mature. The youngsters in this group may resemble the adults in shape and are called nymphs. Because they develop gradually into the adult form their metamorphosis is said to be partial or incomplete. Insects with this type of life history include mayflies, dragonflies, stoneflies, grasshoppers and crickets, earwigs, cockroaches, mantids, stick insects, psocids, bugs and thrips. The lice are also included here, although they have no wings, because they are clearly related to other members of the group. Being wingless, they grow up with very little change in their appearance.

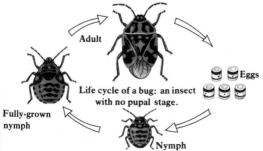

Adult

Eggs

Life cycle of a bug: an insect with no pupal stage.

Fully-grown nymph

Nymph

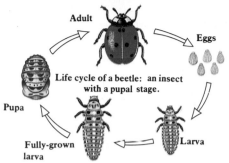

Adult

Eggs

Life cycle of a beetle: an insect with a pupal stage.

Pupa

Fully-grown larva

Larva

Youngsters of the second group are called larvae and, as you can see from the ladybird life cycle, they look nothing like the adults. They often lack legs as well as wings. The larva may change colour when it moults, but there is no sign of wing buds: it merely becomes a bigger larva. When fully grown it moults again, but not to reveal the adult. An extra stage is inserted in this type of life history. Known as the pupa or chrysalis, it does not feed and rarely moves. Great changes take place inside it as the larval body is converted into that of the adult. The outlines of legs, wings and even antennae are usually visible on the pupal surface. When the changes are complete the adult bursts out of the pupal skin. This kind of life history, with a very abrupt change of form, is known as complete metamorphosis. Insects growing up in this way include lacewings, scorpion flies, true flies, fleas, butterflies and moths, caddis flies, bees and wasps, ants and beetles.

Camouflage and mimicry

Insects have many enemies, including birds, lizards, small mammals, spiders and other insects. Not suprisingly, they have evolved various ways of protecting themselves, although their defences obviously do not work against all enemies. Quick reactions enable many insects to escape from approaching enemies, as you will know if you have ever tried to swat a fly, but it is even better to avoid detection altogether. Many insects are extremely good at this and their camouflage takes many different forms. Grasshoppers and some of the bush crickets blend beautifully with their leafy surroundings and are hard to spot even when you can hear them chirping in front of you. Stick insects and many caterpillars look just like twigs, while some of the treehoppers can be mistaken for buds or even prickles. Some resting moths look just like dead and shrivelled leaves, and some even resemble bird droppings – a marvellous way of avoiding the attentions of birds. Some insects actively disguise themselves. Many caddis fly larvae, for example, build cases of sand or plant fragments around themselves, while the larvae of some lacewings cover themselves with plant debris and the skins of their aphid victims. The larva of the green tortoise beetle covers itself with its own droppings and then looks just like a bird dropping sitting on a leaf.

A different form of camouflage or deception is employed by those insects that bluff their way out of trouble by 'pretending' to be larger or fiercer than they really are. The eyed hawkmoth is one of the best examples, displaying the face of an owl or cat – much to the alarm of inquisitive small birds. The praying mantis also uses bluff to scare birds and lizards (*see page 59*), and it puts on the same hissing display when prodded by the inquisitive naturalist.

Only a few insects possess real weapons, the best known being the stings of bees and wasps and many ants. The stings are modified ovipositors, so only females can sting. Many of those ants without stings, including the wood ant, can fire formic acid at their attackers, and the bombardier beetle (*see page 173*) can also fire caustic fluids when attacked.

Many insects have foul-tasting flesh or fluids, or irritating hairs which make them unpalatable to birds and other enemies. This in itself does not prevent their being attacked, because the unpleasantness is not felt until afterwards, but most of the unpalatable insects sport bold or even gaudy patterns, known as warning colours. Birds and other predators are quick to associate these colours with unpleasant experiences and thereafter leave the insects alone. Black and yellow is a common warning combination, used by most wasps to advertise their stings and their acrid tastes. Black and red is also very common, being employed by the burnets and various other moths and also by many bugs (*see page 68*).

Not all boldy marked insects are unpalatable. Many harmless and edible species resemble the unpleasant ones and escape attack as a result. This phenomenon is called mimicry, with the unpleasant species known as the model and its harmless imitator the mimic.

Some mimics' resemblances are extremely close, while others are only superficial, but even a passing resemblance may be enough to make a bird hesitate and give the insect time to escape. Wasps are some of the commonest models, and the hover-flies (*pages 122-7*) are among their commonest mimics.

All forms of camouflage and mimicry – which are both types of deception – have evolved by means of natural selection. Predators continually select and remove the least well camouflaged individuals or the least effective mimics, leaving the best ones to breed. The camouflage or mimicry thus gradually improves, although many generations are needed to convert a passing resemblance into a spitting image.

The classification of insects

The insects are arranged in 29 groups, known as orders, although some entomologists prefer to split some of these groups and thus create more orders. The nature of the wings and the form of the jaws are the main features involved in grouping the insects and most of the order names end in ...ptera, which means 'wings'. The caddis flies, for example, belong to the order Trichoptera, which means 'hairy wings', for the wings of these insects are clothed with minute hairs. Apart from the Lepidoptera (butterflies and moths), which are not featured in this book, but in a companion volume, the major orders found in Europe are listed on pages 3-4.

The other arthropods

The four other major groups or classes of arthropods are the arachnids, the chilopods, the diplopods and the crustaceans. Although none of these ever has any wings, they are often confused with insects and a representative selection is therefore included at the end of the book (*pages 214-33*).

The arachnids include the spiders and scorpions and their relatives and they differ from the insects in having four pairs of walking legs. There are no antennae, although many of these creatures have sensory palps that look and behave like antennae. The chilopods are the centipedes, predatory arthropods with clearly segmented, elongate bodies and a pair of legs on each segment. The diplopods are the millipedes, vegetarian creatures often resembling the centipedes but with more cylindrical bodies and with two pairs of legs on most of the segments. The crustaceans include the crabs and shrimps and their relatives. Almost all of them live in water and the only land-living examples are the woodlice. The latter all have seven pairs of legs.

A word about names

English names are used here whenever possible, but only the most familiar insects have these common names. The rest have only Latin names, but these are understood by biologists the world over. Each has two parts – a generic name, always given a capital letter, and a specific name. Closely related creatures share the same generic name.

PRIMITIVE WINGLESS INSECTS

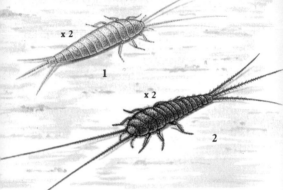

The insects shown here have no wings at any stage and are collectively known as Apterygotes.

1 Silverfish (*Lepisma saccharina*) Clothed with silvery scales, this insect lives mainly in houses and feeds on starchy materials. Like the next two species, it belongs to the group known as bristletails.

2 Firebrat (*Thermobia domestica*) likes warmer places than the silverfish. You are most likely to find it in bakeries and large kitchens.

3 *Petrobius maritimus* lives in rock crevices and under stones by the sea. It feeds at night on seaweeds and assorted debris.

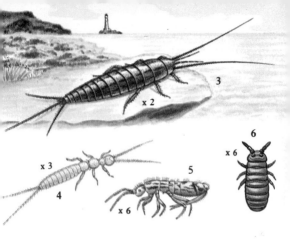

x 2

x 3

x 6

x 6

4 *Campodea staphylinus* lives and feeds in decaying vegetation. It belongs to the group called two-pronged bristletails. Look for it in compost heaps.

5 *Orchesella villosa* is one of the springtails, so called for the forked spring at the rear. Normally tucked under the body, the spring is released and shoots the insect forward when it is alarmed. Many kinds of springtail live in moss and leaf litter, feeding on minute plant fragments.

6 *Podura aquatica* is a tiny springtail living on the surface of ponds, often in huge swarms. It feeds on pollen and other minute debris.

MAYFLIES

Mayflies are delicate insects, rarely found far from the water in which they spend their early lives. Some species have three tails, others only two. Some have no hind wings. The wings are held vertically over the body at rest, as in butterflies. The winged adults which emerge from the mature nymphs are dull and hairy and called duns. They are not fully mature and, unlike any other winged insects, they undergo another moult: a fine skin peels away from the whole body, including the wings, revealing the shiny, short-lived full adult or spinner.

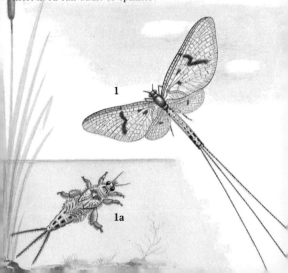

1

1a

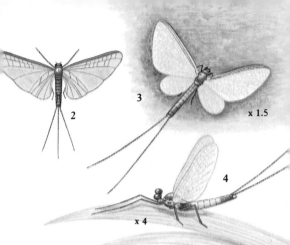

1 Ephemera danica is the largest British mayfly. Its nymph (**1a**) lives in the mud of still and slow-moving water, feeding on algae and debris.

2 Oligoneuriella rhenana swarms over large rivers in summer in southern and central Europe. Not found in Britain.

3 Ephoron virgo is easily identified by its white wings. It often swarms around lights near the water in southern and central Europe. Not found in Britain.

4 Centroptilum luteolum has very narrow hind wings. Like many mayflies, the male has large flat-topped eyes.

DRAGONFLIES

Dragonflies are generally fast-flying and very agile insects, catching midges and other small flies in mid-air for food. Huge eyes help them to spot their prey, which they scoop up with their spiny legs. Dragonflies have no sting and are harmless to humans. During mating, the male grasps the female's neck with the tip of his abdomen and she then curves her body round to collect sperm from near the front of his abdomen (see *page 32*). She then either scatters her eggs freely in the water or lays them in slits and crevices in submerged plants. She may still be held by the male while doing this. The nymphs feed on a wide range of small water creatures. When fully grown they climb waterside plants and their skins split open for the adults to emerge.

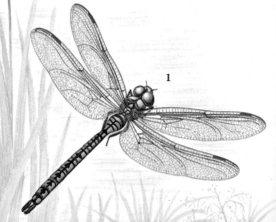

1

they climb waterside plants and their skins split open for the adults to emerge.

1 Emperor Dragonfly (*Anax imperator*) is bright blue in the male and greenish blue in the female, although, as in all dragonflies, the colours take several days to develop fully. Absent from northern Europe.

2 Brown Aeshna (*Aeshna grandis*), seen here laying eggs on a submerged plant, is Europe's only common brown-winged species. Notice the wing buds developing on the back of the nymph (**2a**).

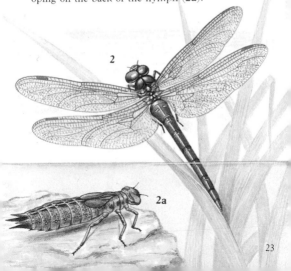

1

2

24

DRAGONFLIES contd.

1 *Aeshna cyanea* is distinguished from several similarly coloured species by the broad green stripes on the thorax. It breeds mainly in still ponds, but adults can be found far from any water.

2 Gold-ringed Dragonfly (*Cordulegaster boltonii*) occurs mainly on heaths and moors. the female lays her eggs in gravel on stream beds.

3 *Orthetrum cancellatum* is black and yellow when young, but the male's abdomen becomes blue when fully mature. The stigma near the wing-tip is black. All the dragonflies described so far have been 'hawkers', spending long hours hawking to and fro in search of food, but *Orthetrum* is one of the 'darters', related to those on the next page.

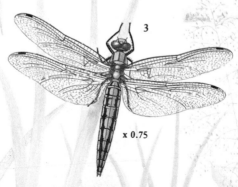

3

x 0.75

DARTER DRAGONFLIES

The dragonflies on this page are all 'darters': instead of hawking to and fro in search of prey, they prefer to sit on a convenient perch, dart out when prey approaches, and then return to the perch.

1 *Libellula depressa* has a blue abdomen only in the fully mature male: females and young males are brown with yellow spots on the sides. All four wings always have a dark base.

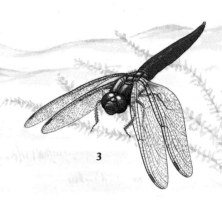

3

2 Libellula quadrimaculata is easily recognised by the dark spot about half way along the front edge of each wing. The male never becomes blue. Found mainly on heaths and moors, this is a great migrant. Swarms containing millions of insects are sometimes seen, especially in Scandinavia, where the numerous lakes provide excellent breeding sites for the insect.

3 Crocothemis erythraea, seen here in the darter's hot-weather pose with wings pulled down to shade the thorax, is yellow or brown at first, but its body soon becomes bright red. The veins at the front of each wing are also red. It is a southern species, absent from Britain.

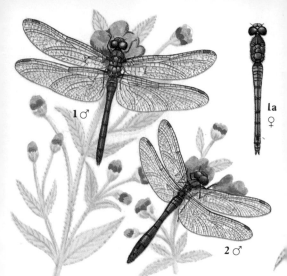

1 ♂

1a
♀

2 ♂

DARTER DRAGONFLIES contd.

1 Sympetrum striolatum, like all *Sympetrum* species, is a rather slender darter. Male is much redder than the female (**1a**). Continental specimens tend to be larger and paler.

2 Sympetrum sanguineum male has a clubbed abdomen and is crimson red when fully mature. Female is like that of the previous species but has completely black legs with no yellow stripe. It breeds mainly in swampy places.

3 *Sympetrum flaveolum* is easily recognised by the large yellow patch on the hind wing, together with a reddish stigma. Like its relatives, it is a strong migrant. Although not resident in the northern half of Europe, it is a summer visitor from the south.

4 *Leucorrhinia caudalis* has a swollen abdomen in both sexes, but only the mature male has any blue. The stigma is darker brown in females. It is a central European species not found in Britain.

DAMSELFLIES

The damselflies belong to the same order as the dragonflies, but are much more slender and delicate and they fly much more slowly. They pluck much of their prey from the waterside plants. Unlike dragonflies, they can fold their wings together and hold them vertically above the body at rest. All four wings are the same size. The life history is similar to that of dragonflies, although the eggs are nearly always laid in the stems of water plants. The male usually holds the female while she is egg-laying and may lower her completely into the water while clinging to a reed. The nymphs (**2b**) are more slender than those of dragonflies and have three leaf-like gills at the hind end.

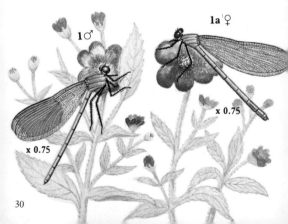

1a ♀

1♂

x 0.75

x 0.75

1 Agrion splendens male has a metallic blue or green body. The wing patch is brown at first but then becomes deep blue. It may extend right to the wing-tip. Female (**1a**) is always green, with greenish wings. It likes canals and quiet, muddy rivers.

2 Agrion virgo male has virtually all the wing bluish. Female (**2a**) always has a green body and brown wings when mature. It prefers faster streams with sandy bottoms.

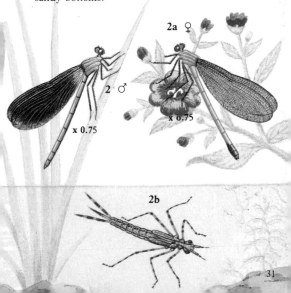

2a ♀

2 ♂

x 0.75

x 0.75

2b

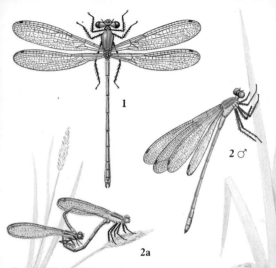

1

2 ♂

2a

DAMSELFLIES contd.

1 *Lestes barbarus* is one of the largest of the European damselflies and is easily recognised by its bright green body and the two-coloured stigma near each wing-tip. Notice the male's large claspers, used for grasping the female during mating. It is common in the Mediterranean area, where it is often breeds in brackish pools along the coast, but scattered colonies also occur in central Europe. It does not live in Britain.

2 Lestes sponsa develops blue patches only in the mature male. The mating position (**2a**), typical of all Odonata, is known as the copulation wheel. The insects usually rest on the vegetation while mating, but they can also fly in this position. *L. sponsa* breeds in ponds, including those on heathland, with plenty of fringing vegetation.

3 Platycnemis pennipes can be distinguished from other blue damselflies (*pages 34-5*) by its broad white middle and hind legs which, on close inspection, will be seen to have a thin black stripe on them. Female body is very pale greenish blue and sometimes almost white. It breeds in still and slow-moving water.

3

DAMSELFLIES contd.

1 *Enallagma cyathigerum* is one of the commonest damselflies. Male is easily recognised by the small black mark, like the ace of spades, at the front of abdomen. Female is darker and less easy to distinguish, but has a conspicuous spine under 8th abdominal segment. It breeds in all kinds of still and slow-moving water, where pairs can often be seen flying in tandem (**1a**) in search of egg-laying sites.

2 Coenagrion puella is another very common blue species, whose male has a U-shaped mark at front of abdomen. Female (**2a**), when fresh, can be identified by a wine-glass-shaped mark at front of abdomen.

3 Ischnura elegans is one of the smaller species, identified by a blue patch at the rear end and by the bi-coloured stigma. There is a small upright spine just behind the head.

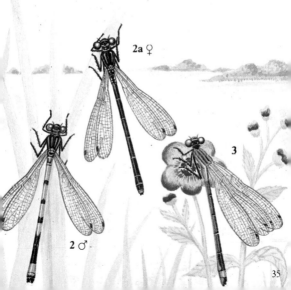

2a ♀

2 ♂

3

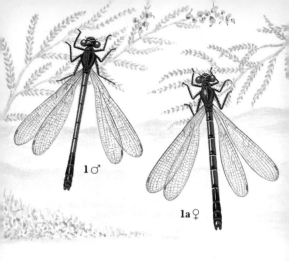

1 ♂

1a ♀

DAMSELFLIES contd.

1 Large Red Damselfly (*Pyrrhosoma nymphula*) is one of the few red species. Look for red stripes on the thorax and completely black legs. Female (**1a**) has much more black on body. Breeds in still and slow-moving water: often common on peat bogs and may fly as early as mid-April. As with all dragonflies and damselflies, the full colour takes several days to develop.

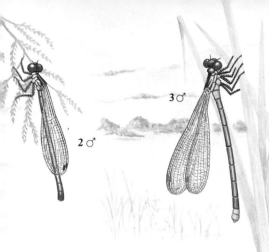

2 Small Red Damselfly (*Ceriagrion tenellum*) has red legs and no red stripes on the thorax. Female abdomen is bronzy black. Southern and central Europe, mostly on acidic bogs and marshes.

3 Red-eyed Damselfly (*Erythromma najas*) has prominent red eyes and no coloured spots on the head. Female has no blue tip to abdomen. Close inspection will reveal a denser network of veins near the tip of the hind wing than near that of the front wing. This relatively sturdy and fast-flying damselfly likes still and slow-moving water with plenty of floating vegetation on which to rest.

STONEFLIES

Stoneflies are all rather drab, greyish brown or yellowish insects, usually found close to clear lakes and streams. The nymphs (**2a**) live in the water, some eating small animals and others nibbling plants. They are generally flattened, with two tails and large claws with which they cling to stones or vegetation. They leave the water when fully grown and the adults emerge through a slit in the back, leaving the empty nymphal skins (**3a**) on the stones. The adults fly little and few even feed, although some may nibble algae and pollen.

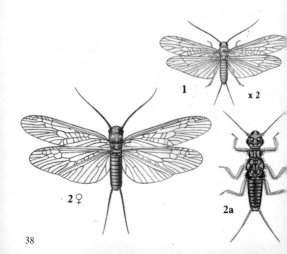

1   x 2

2 ♀

2a

1 _Isoperla grammatica_ is the only large yellow species in Britain, although several occur on the continent. It likes stony lowland streams, especially in limestone areas.

2 _Perlodes microcephala_ is distinguished from most other large species by the irregular network of veins near the wing-tip. Male has very short wings and cannot fly. It breeds in stony lowland streams in southern and central Europe. Several similar species live in European mountains.

3 _Dinocras cephalotes_ male is only half the size of female shown here. Thorax always black. It breeds in rivers with large, moss-covered stones on bottom: mainly in uplands.

3 ♀

3a

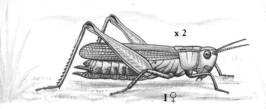

x 2

1 ♀

GRASSHOPPERS

These sprightly, sun-loving insects live mainly in rough grassland and are best known for their chirpy songs, which they make by rubbing their hind legs against the forewings. Generally only the males sing, and each species has its own song to attract the right kind of mate. Many fly well, but some have short wings and are flightless. Most jump well with their long back legs. They feed almost entirely on grass. Eggs are laid in the ground and most European species spend the winter in the egg stage. The nymphs look like small adults with stumpy wings, but can be distinguished from short-winged adults because the wing buds are turned in the older nymphs so that the straight edge is at the top instead of along the side (*see page 49*). Colours are very variable and the songs are often a better guide to identification.

1 Common Green Grasshopper (*Omocestus viridulus*) likes rather lush grassland and is predominantly green, although brown forms do occur. Song: up to 20 seconds, starting very quietly and gradually getting louder before stopping abruptly.

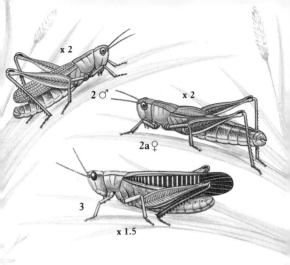

2 Meadow Grasshopper (*Chorthippus parallelus*) is Britain's only flightless species. The forewings are short, especially in the female (**2a**) and the hind wings are virtually absent. It is mainly green, but sometimes brown or purple. Song: lasts no more than 3 seconds, during which time it gets gradually louder, and is repeated at irregular intervals.

3 *Chorthippus scalaris* is a very noisy insect, with a loud, buzzing song and rustling flight. Male forewings are very broad. Green or brown, it is a mountain insect and not found in Britain.

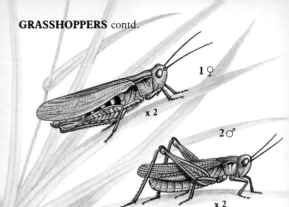

1 Common Field Grasshopper (*Chorthippus brunneus*) may also be green, grey or black. It is always very hairy under the thorax and, like all *Chorthippus* species, it has a small bulge on the front edge of the forewing. It likes relatively dry grassland. Song: a succession of 6-10 short chirps.

2 *Chorthippus biguttulus* is like the last species but the forewing is strongly curved, especially in male. Song: a loud, metallic chirp lasting about 1.5 seconds. Not found in Britain.

3 Lesser Marsh Grasshopper (*Chorthippus albomarginatus*) is green or brown and lives in both dry and damp grassland. The keels at the top of the thorax are almost straight. Song: 2-6 short chirps, each separated by about 2 seconds.

4 Stripe-winged Grasshopper (*Stenobothrus lineatus*) likes dry grassland. There are prominent parallel cross veins in the central area of the forewing. Male lacks white stripe. Song: a high-pitched whine, rising and falling in volume. Southern and central Europe.

5 Mottled Grasshopper (*Myrmeleotettix maculatus*) is a very small species with lighty clubbed antennae. Dry places, including heathland. Song: up to 30 short chirps in about 15 seconds, rather like the sound of winding up a watch or clock.

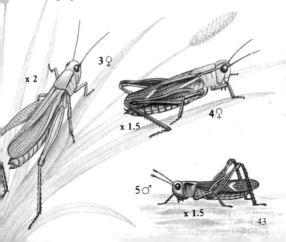

GRASSHOPPERS contd.

1 Euthystira brachyptera is a flightless species with short wings in both sexes and a silky lustre to its body. Female (**1a**) is much longer than male. It lives in mountain grassland where the turf is short and stony. Song: a succession of short buzzes, rather like someone striking matches. Southern and central Europe. Not found in Britain.

2 Podisma pedestris is another flightless montane species, often found in sparsely vegetated areas near the snow-line. The heavy female can only drag herself over the ground or vegetation. No song. Not found in Britain. The very similar *Podisma alpina* has yellowish hind tibiae.

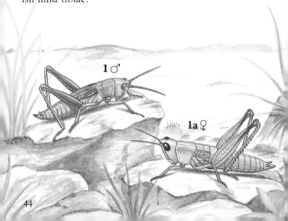

3 Gomphocerus sibiricus male is immediately recognised by its swollen front legs. Female has normal legs and less swollen antennae than male, but the front half of the thorax is clearly raised to form a rounded hump. Song: begins with distinct ticking sounds which gradually speed up and become a constant hiss lasting for as much as a minute. Lives in mountainous regions, mostly in the Alps and Pyrenees: not found in Britain.

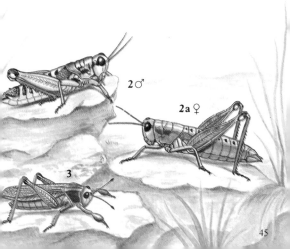

2 ♂

2a ♀

3

GRASSHOPPERS contd.

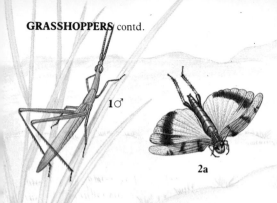

1♂

2a

2

x 1.5

1 *Acrida ungarica* cannot be mistaken for anything else in western Europe because of its shape. It may be green or brown, often with mottled wings. Female is up to 75mm long. No song. Lives in damp grassland in southern Europe.

2 *Oedipoda caerulescens* may be mistaken for a butterfly when displaying its blue hind wings in flight (**2a**), but it is difficult to see on the ground. As in all

Oedipoda species, there is a distinct notch on the hind leg and a prominent groove running across the thorax. No song. It lives in all kinds of dry habitats in southern and central Europe but is not found in Britain.

3 *Oedipoda germanica* is one of several grasshoppers with red hind wings. It lives in the same dry places as the last species but is less common. Absent from Britain and northern Europe.

4 *Arcyptera fusca* lives on montane pastures, mainly in the Alps and Pyrenees. Male flies well, but heavy female has shorter wings and does not fly. Song: loud, consisting of several short notes followed by a warble for about 3 seconds and finishing with 2 or 3 more short notes. It is not found in Britain.

1

GRASSHOPPERS contd.

1 *Calliptamus italicus* is one of several similar stout species, all with a blunt forehead and a peg between the front legs. The pale stripe may be missing from the sides of the thorax and the wings. Female much larger than male, but he has extra-large claspers at the hind end to grip her while mating. No real song. Sometimes a pest of cultivated ground in southern and central Europe. Not found in Britain.

2 Egyptian Grasshopper (*Anacridium aegyptium*) can be recognised by the striped eyes and several indentations of the keel on top of the thorax. There is also a blunt peg between the front legs. Female is up to 65mm long. On various plants all year in southern Europe: sometimes carried north in vegetable produce. Nymph (**2a**) is brown or green. Notice the reversed wing buds, with the front edge lying along the middle of back instead of at sides as in adult. No song.

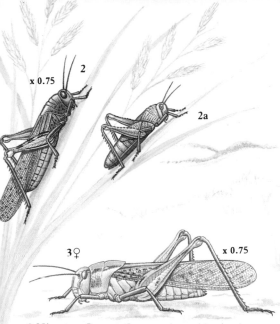

x 0.75

2

2a

3♀   x 0.75

3 Migratory Locust (*Locusta migratoria*) exists in two forms, but only the solitary form shown here is common in Europe. Notice the swollen thorax. Male is smaller and often brown. He screeches loudly in the presence of a female. Found on all kinds of vegetation, especially around Mediterranean, but rarely a pest in Europe. Swarming (gregarious) form is brown or yellow.

49

BUSH CRICKETS

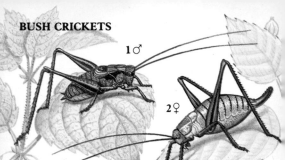

1 ♂

2 ♀

Bush crickets belong to the same order as the grasshopppers but have much longer antennae and males sing by rubbing the bases of their forewings together. The songs are often higher-pitched than those of grasshoppers and may go on for much longer periods. Females have a broad, often sabre-like ovipositor, with which they lay eggs in the ground or in slits in plants. The insects are at least partly carnivorous and, unlike grasshoppers, are often active at night. Many have very short wings and are unable to fly.

1 Dark Bush Cricket (*Pholidoptera griseoaptera*) male has very small wings perched on his back. He produces a staccato chirp from hedgerows and bramble thickets, mainly in the afternoon and evening. Female is paler and wingless.

2 Barbitistes fischeri is bright green when young. Male has wings rather like those of the last species.

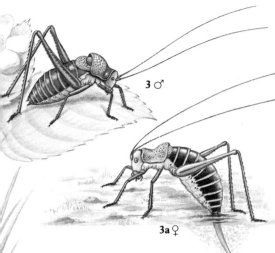

3 ♂

3a ♀

Song: a sequence of 20-40 weak scratching sounds lasting for up to 20 seconds. Confined to southern Europe.

3 *Ephippiger ephippiger* is known as 'le tizi' in France because its high-pitched, two-syllable call, repeated at regular intervals, sounds just like *tizi*. Both sexes sing as they crawl over vegtation. Female lays her eggs in the ground with her long ovipositor (**3a**). Green or brown, it is one of several similar species in southern and central Europe, but not found in Britain.

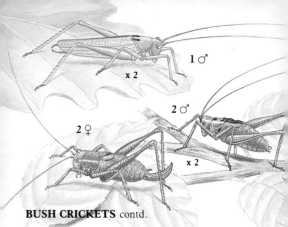

BUSH CRICKETS contd.

1 Oak Bush Cricket (*Meconema thalassinum*) is fully winged in both sexes and often flies to lighted windows on autumn evenings. It lives in various trees, eating a wide range of small insects and nibbling the occasional leaf. Male has very large claspers at rear, while female has a long, curved ovipositor. No song, but male taps the leaves with his hind legs, raising his wings at the same time to direct the sound.

2 Speckled Bush Cricket (*Leptophyes punctatissima*) is flightless and lives among nettles and brambles, where it is very hard to spot. It is also quite common in rural gardens. Song: a weak scratching sound, difficult to detect.

3 *Tylopsis liliifolia* has antennae up to five times its body length. Female ovipositor is very short and strongly curved. The insect is green or brown and lives in rough herbage. Song: 2-4 weak chirps, rather like someone striking matches. Found in southern Europe.

4 Short-winged Conehead (*Conocephalus dorsalis*) has short forewings and no hind wings in both sexes. Although active mainly by day, it is very hard to see among the reeds and tall grasses of its marshland and waterside homes. Song: a prolonged hissing, rising and falling like the sound of a knife-grinder.

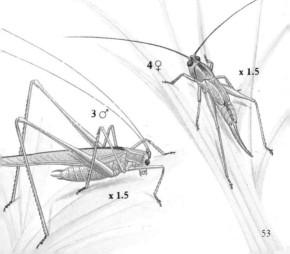

4 ♀

x 1.5

3 ♂

x 1.5

BUSH CRICKETS contd.

1 *Tettigonia cantans* has distinctly rounded fore-wings. Song: a prolonged rasping sound heard mainly at night. It lives chiefly in upland areas. Not found in Britain.

2 Great Green Bush Cricket (*Tettigonia viridissima*) is Britain's largest species, fully winged in both sexes. Forewings much longer than in previous species and reaching the tip of the ovipositor. Song: a prolonged buzzing, less harsh than that of the previous species and sounding somewhat like a sewing machine. Often heard by day, but mostly in the evening. Mainly

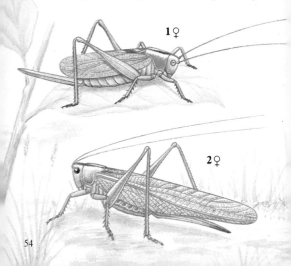

carnivorous, feeding on small insects in rough herbage.

3 Wart Biter (*Decticus verrucivorus*) is another largely carnivorous species and, like the other three species shown here, can give you a painful bite. The Swedes once used the insect to bite off their warts! Female ovipositor extends well beyond wings. It is green or brown, always heavily mottled and lives mainly in grassy places. Song: a prolonged whirring, rather like a free-wheeling bicycle.

4 *Decticus albifrons* has a very pale face. It lives in dry habitats in southern Europe and is active by day. Song: high pitched, beginning with bird-like chirps and then speeding up to produce a harsh ratchet-like sound. It flies well.

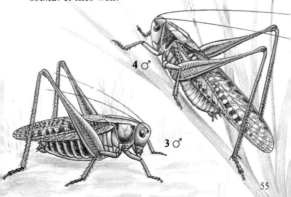

CRICKETS

True crickets differ from bush crickets in having a straight, needle-like ovipositor and feet with three segments instead of four. Most are omnivorous creatures.

1 Field Cricket (*Gryllus campestris*) is flightless, burrowing in grassy places and coming out by day and night. Song: a shrill warble, consisting of 3-4 chirps per second, delivered from the burrow entrance. Absent from northern Europe.

2 Mole Cricket (*Gryllotalpa gryllotalpa*) spends most of its time tunnelling in damp meadows with its huge front legs. It feeds on roots and various insects. It may fly on warm evenings. Song: a quiet churring produced at the burrow entrance. The female has no visible ovipositor. It is not closely related to the other crickets.

3 Italian Cricket (*Oecanthus pellucens*) lives in trees and all kinds of rough herbage. Female has much narrower wings. Song: a delicate warble – *grii-grii-grii* – produced mainly at night with wings raised up above body. The insect alters the volume when disturbed, so that the sound appears to come from a different place, It lives in the southern half of Europe.

4 House Cricket (*Acheta domesticus*) is fully winged. Rolled-up hind wings project like extra tails at rest. Found mostly in buildings, but also on rubbish dumps. Mainly nocturnal. Song: a shrill, prolonged, bird-like warble.

5 *Gryllomorpha dalmatina* is a wingless and silent species, often found in and around buildings in southern Europe.

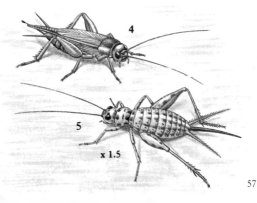

x 1.5

STICK INSECTS & MANTIDS

1 *Clonopsis gallicus* is one of about five species of stick insects which live in southern Europe. It is completely wingless and feeds on a wide range of plants. Males are rare and females lay fertile eggs without mating. (*Bacillus rossius* is similar but has longer antennae.)

MANTIDS catch other insects with lightning-fast movements of their spiky front legs. Eggs are laid in masses of froth which soon become hard and horny. Most species pass the winter in the egg stage. None lives in Britain or northern Europe.

2 *Ameles decolor* is one of several similar small mantids in southern Europe. Female is plumper and flightless, with very short wings.

3 *Empusa pennata* is immediately recognised by its long neck. It may be green or brown. The nymph generally folds its abdomen forward over the thorax (**3a**). It passes the winter as a nymph.

4 *Mantis religiosa* is the original praying mantis, so called because of the way it holds its 'arms' in front of its face. Brown or green, it lives amongst all kinds of low-growing vegetation. Male is more slender and is often eaten by the female during mating. When alarmed, the insect puts on a threat display, revealing imitation eyes and making hissing sounds by rubbing its abdomen against its wings (**4a**).

COCKROACHES

Cockroaches belong to the same order as the mantids, although they behave quite differently. They are fast-running scavengers, active mainly at night and hiding in crevices by day. Several small species live in the wild in Europe, but the best known are the imported species which have become pests in buildings, especially warehouses, kitchens, and other permanently heated premises. Eggs are laid in horny 'purses' which the female may carry around with her for several days. Apart from the lack of wings, the nymphs are very like the adults.

1 American Cockroach (*Periplaneta americana*) is fully winged and is common in many large buildings and also on ships. Despite its name, it probably came originally from Africa.

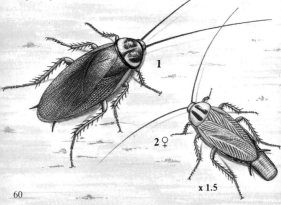

1

2 ♀

x 1.5

2 German Cockroach (*Blatella germanica*), seen here carrying its egg purse, also comes from Africa. It is found in buildings and also on rubbish dumps, where the fermenting rubbish provides warmth. It has wings but rarely flies.

3 Common Cockroach (*Blatta orientalis*) is flightless, with female (**3a**) virtually wingless. Its original home is unknown, but it now occurs in buildings and on rubbish dumps.

4 Tawny Cockroach (*Ectobius pallidus*) is fully winged in both sexes and found mainly in woods and rough grassland. It is a native of southern and central Europe.

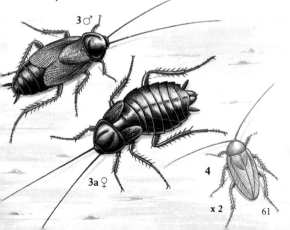

3♂

3a ♀

4

x 2

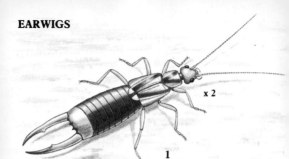

x 2

1

Earwigs are easily recognised by the pincers, generally stouter and more curved in males than in females. Males sometimes wrestle with their pincers when disputing food or females, but the pincers are used mainly for defence against shrews and similar enemies. They are harmless to us. The forewings are short and horny in the four British species, but are absent in many continental species. Hind wings, when present, are very flimsy and elaborately folded under the forewings. Fully winged species can fly, but few do so readily. Earwigs are scavengers, active mainly by night and hiding in crevices by day.

1 *Labidura riparia* is Europe's largest earwig, rarely found far from the coast and often living right on the sea shore. Not found in Britain or northern Europe.

2 Forficula auricularia is Europe's commonest species, found almost everywhere. It is fully winged, with tips of hind wings protruding from under forewings. As in all species, the female tends her eggs, often for several months, and continually licks them to keep them clean (**2a**). She also feeds the nymphs for a while. Nymphs are like adults, but without wings and with very slender pincers. White earwigs (**2b**) are often unearthed. These are merely individuals which have just moulted and whose new coats have not yet hardened.

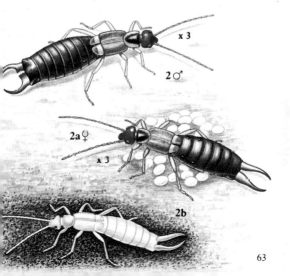

x 3

2♂

2a♀

x 3

2b

BUGS

The bugs form the very large order Hemiptera, characterised by piercing beaks (*see picture*) used for sucking the juices of other animals or plants. When not in use, the beak is folded back under the head and may extend right back between the legs. There are two very distinct sub-orders – the Heteroptera (*pages 64-81*) and the Homoptera (*pages 82-91*). The Heteroptera include both herbivorous and carnivorous species and the forewings, when present, have a horny base and a membranous tip. This structure, together with the beak, easily separates the bugs from the beetles. Hind wings, when present, are always membranous. The Homoptera are all plant-feeders and the forewings, when present, are completely horny or leathery or else completely membranous.

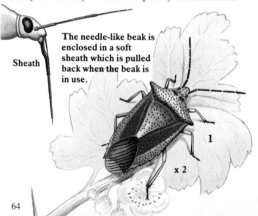

The needle-like beak is enclosed in a soft sheath which is pulled back when the beak is in use.

Sheath

1

x 2

1 Hawthorn Shield Bug (*Acanthosoma haemorrhoidale*) feeds mainly on hawthorn leaves and fruits. It is one of many species known as shield bugs for their shape. Many are also called stink bugs because, when handled or otherwise disturbed, they emit pungent fluids. Most of them hibernate as adults.

2 Pied Shield Bug (*Sehirus bicolor*) lives on dead-nettles and is common in hedgerows in spring and autumn. The adults hibernate in the ground.

3 Parent Bug (*Elasmucha grisea*) gets its name because the female sits guard over her eggs when she has laid them on a birch leaf. She also guards the young nymphs for a few days.

SHIELD BUGS

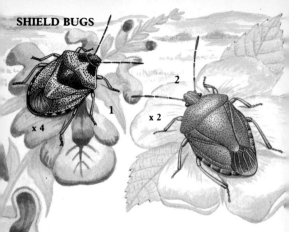

1 *Eysarcoris fabricii* is one of the smaller shield bugs and has a pattern of shining bronze or purplish markings on a greyish background. It lives and feeds on hedge woundwort, often gathering in huge numbers.

2 Green Shield Bug (*Palomena prasina*) is one of several entirely green shield bugs, although the only one normally found in Britain. It is bright green in spring and summer, becoming bronze as it prepares for hibernation in late autumn. It feeds on a wide range of plants and is sometimes a crop pest on the continent where, like the shield bugs as a whole, it is much more common.

3 Nezara viridula is very like the previous species but often develops pale brown patches on the head and thorax. The membranous wing-tips are paler than in the previous species. Its colourful nymph (**3a**) is especially noticeable on herbage in late summer. It exhibits the typical rounded shape of the shield bug nymphs. Both adult and nymph cause considerable damage to potatoes and other crops. Not found in Britain or northern Europe.

4 Carpocoris fuscispinus is abundant on the continent and has two forms – the one with a sharp-angled thorax shown here and one with rounder angles. Both forms occur in the south, but only the sharp-angled form occurs in the north. It feeds on a wide range of plants. Not found in Britain.

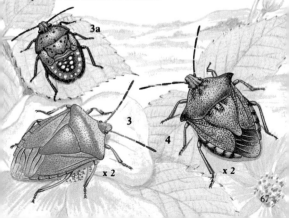

SHIELD BUGS contd.

1 *Graphosoma italicum* has a particularly foul taste and advertises the fact with its bold colours. Birds soon learn to leave it alone. The scutellum reaches virtually to the tip of the body, covering most of the wings as well as the abdomen. Abundant in the southern half of Europe, it is especially common on umbellifer flowers. Not found in Britain. (*Graphosoma semipunctatum* is very similar but has spots instead of stripes on the thorax and its legs are mainly red.)

2 European Tortoise Bug (*Eurygaster maura*) ranges from pale brown to black and has an enormous scutellum covering the wings and reaching the tip of the abdomen. It lives in dense grassland and feeds mainly on the grasses. It is sometimes a pest of cereals on the continent. There are several similar species.

3 *Eurydema dominulus* has a variable black pattern on an orange or red background. Feeding on a wide range of cruciferous plants, it is rare in Britain but a considerable pest of cabbages and other brassicas on the continent.

4 Brassica Bug (*Eurydema oleracea*) is a shiny blue-black or greenish black bug with variable white, yellow or reddish markings. Food plants include many crucifers, such as garlic mustard. It is not common in Britain, but a serious pest of brassicas and vines on the continent.

x 3

1

2

x 3

x 3

3

x 3

4

69

BUGS contd.

1 Picromerus bidens is a predatory shield bug, easily recognised by the strong thoracic spines. It lives amongst lush vegetation, especially in damp hedgerows and woodland clearings, feeding mainly on caterpillars and beetle grubs. It passes the winter in the egg stage.

2 Forest Bug (*Pentatoma rufipes*) resembles the last species but lacks the sharp spines. It lives in a wide variety of trees, including garden apples and cherries, feeding on caterpillars and probably some fruit. It hibernates as a nymph.

1

2

x 2

x 2

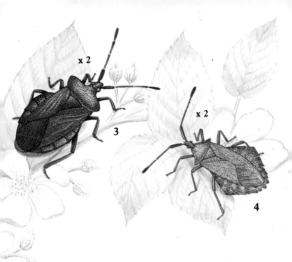

x 2

3

x 2

4

3 *Coreus marginatus* belongs to a group known as squash bugs. As in most bugs, the antennae have four segments (instead of the five seen in the shield bugs). It lives on waste ground and in hedgerows, feeding on the leaves and young seeds of docks and their relatives. It hibernates as an adult.

4 *Verlusia rhombea* is a relative of the last species but easily distinguished by its diamond-shaped abdomen. It likes well-drained places with plenty of ground vegetation, feeding on plants in the family Caryophyllaceae and hibernating as an adult.

BUGS contd.

1 *Lygaeus saxatilis* is common in southern and central Europe but does not occur in Britain. Together with the next species, it belongs to a group known as ground bugs. They spend a lot of their time roaming over the ground and mosses in search of vegetable food. They feed on a wide range of plants, with seeds making up a considerable portion of the diet. The bugs often hibernate in dense masses under stones and fallen leaves.

2 *Lygaeus equestris* is distinguished from the last species and several other similar bugs by the white markings on the wing membrane. It lives in southern and central Europe but only occasional specimens reach Britain.

3 Fire Bug (*Pyrrhocoris apterus*) is often found with the last two species, although it is not related to them. It is generally short-winged, as shown here, but

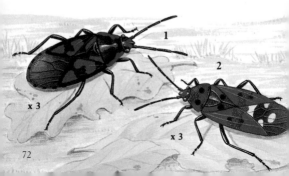

occasionally has fully developed wings. It feeds on a wide range of seeds and other plant materials and you can often see enormous numbers scurrying through the dead leaves on the ground in spring. It is abundant on the continent, but very rare in Britain.

4 *Alydus calcaratus* lives on sandy heaths and readily takes flight in warm weather, revealing a bright orange or red patch on its abdomen (**4a**). When flying fast it can be mistaken for a sand wasp (*page 153*). It feeds largely on seeds. The nymph is ant-like and is often found in ant nests, where it may eat some of the ant grubs but probably exists mainly as a scavenger.

PREDATORY BUGS

1 *Rhinocoris iracundus* stalks and captures a variety of other insects and sucks them dry with its stout, curved beak. Although fully winged, it rarely flies. One of several similar bugs on the continent, it is not found in Britain.

2 *Reduvius personatus* ranges from brown to black and captures a variety of other insects for food. It may 'stab' you and cause considerable pain if you pick it up. It lives in hollow trees, stables and other buildings, where the nymph lives in debris of all kinds. Adults may fly to lighted windows on summer evenings. It passes the winter as a nymph.

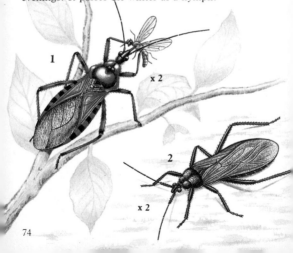

1

x 2

2

x 2

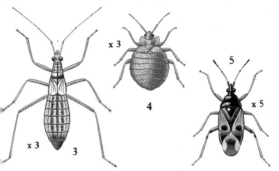

3 Marsh Damsel Bug (*Dolichonabis limbatus*) hunts other insects on the ground and on the vegetation in damp places. It is generally flightless, but fully-winged specimens occasionally appear. It passes the winter in the egg stage.

4 Bed Bug (*Cimex lectularius*) is a wingless blood-sucker, attacking man and other warm-blooded animals. It is quite common in zoos. Hiding in crevices by day, it emerges to feed at night – thus attacking us mainly when we are in bed, although it does not generally spend all day in bed. Better hygiene and the use of insecticides have reduced its numbers in recent years.

5 Common Flower Bug (*Anthocoris nemorum*) is abundant on all kinds of vegetation, eating a wide variety of insects and other small creatures. It hibernates as an adult.

BUGS contd.

1 ***Myrmecoris gracilis*** is a fascinating ant mimic living on grassy heathland. It feeds largely on aphids but may also eat ants' eggs and pupae: it is often found in ant nests. Its straight antennae distinguish it from the ants at a glance.

2 Common Green Capsid (*Lygocoris pabulinus*) is one of several green bugs and is abundant on all kinds of vegetation. The eggs pass the winter on trees and shrubs and the nymphs feed there for a while before dropping down to the herbaceous plants where they complete their growth and often produce a second generation. This bug is a pest of raspberries and other fruits and also damages potato leaves.

3 ***Heterotoma merioptera*** easily identified by its antennae, is common in dense herbage where it feeds mainly on aphids. The eggs overwinter and produce red nymphs in spring.

4 Tarnished Plant Bug (*Lygus rugulipennis*) is one of Europe's commonest bugs, living on a very wide

x 4   1

range of shrubs and herbaceous plants. It is particularly common in the autumn, and then it hibernates as an adult amongst dead leaves.

5 *Leptopterna dolabrata* females are generally short-winged. Common in grassy places, as long as they are not too dry. It sucks sap from grass leaves and flowers and is a minor pest of cereals.

WATER BUGS

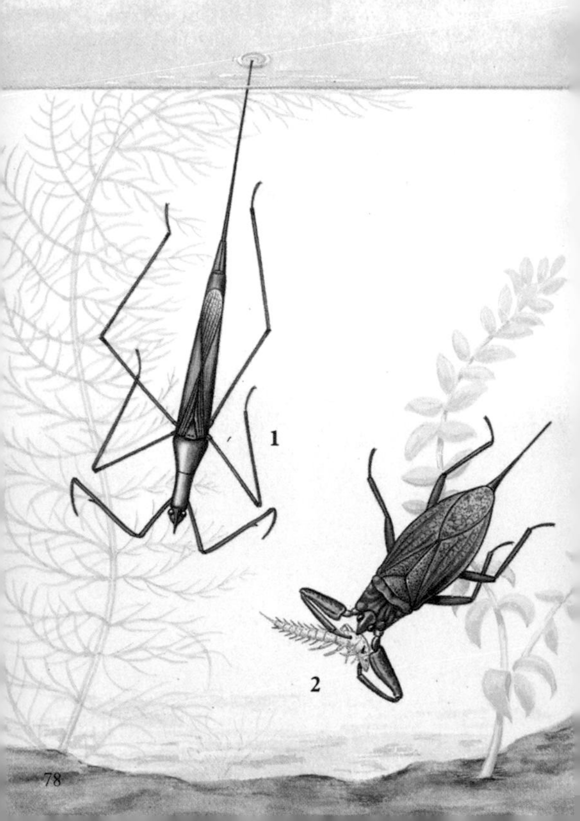

The water bugs all belong to the sub-order Heteroptera (*see page 64*), although they are members of several different families, and they live either in the water or on the surface film. Most are predatory insects. With a few exceptions, they are all airbreathers and most of those living under water must surface periodically to renew their oxygen supplies. Air is carried either under the horny forewings or trapped by a coat of fine hairs on the underside of the body.

1 Water Stick Insect (*Ranatra linearis*) likes deep pools with plenty of submerged vegetation. It remains motionless, clinging to the plants, for long periods while waiting for tadpoles and other small animals to come within range of the grasping front legs. At other times it crawls over the plants or swims in the open water. In sunny weather it will take to the air, especially if the pond is beginning to dry up. The 'tail' is a hollow breathing tube which is periodically pushed up to the surface to draw air into the space beneath the wings.

2 Water Scorpion (*Nepa cinerea*) is harmless in spite of its name and sinister appearance. It lives on the bottom of shallow ponds, where it merges very effectively with the dead leaves. the large front legs are used for catching various small animals. The wing musculature is poorly developed and the insects rarely fly.

WATER BUGS contd.

1 Pond Skater (*Gerris lacustris*) can be seen skimming over still and slow-moving water, feeding on flies and other insects unfortunate enough to fall in. Look for the dimples made by its feet. Each foot is surrounded by water-repellent hairs which prevent it from piercing the surface film. Some have fully-formed wings and fly well, others are flightless.

2 Water Measurer (*Hydrometra stagnorum*) cannot fly and walks slowly over the surface at the edges of ponds and streams. It uses its slender beak to spear small creatures on or just under the surface.

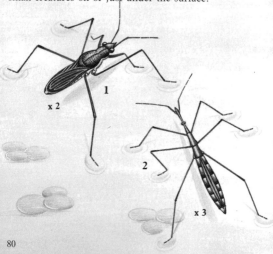

x 2

1

2

x 3

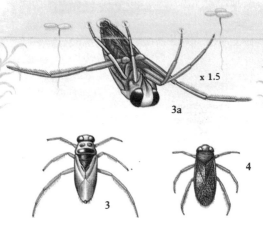

3 Common Backswimmer (*Notonecta glauca*) is one of several bugs that swim upside-down. Its back is strongly keeled, just like a boat, and it rows through the water with its long back legs. It hangs from the surface (**3a**) to renew its air supply, which is held by fine hairs on the belly, giving the insect a silvery appearance under the water. It attacks all kinds of pond creatures.

4 Common Water Boatman (*Corixa punctata*) looks like a backswimmer, but does not swim on its back and has shorter hind legs. It feeds mainly on debris on the bottom of the pond. Adult males chirp loudly, and you can hear this if you put the insects in a shallow dish.

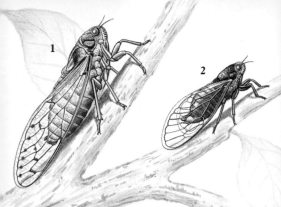

CICADAS & HOPPERS

Cicadas are quite large homopteran bugs (*see page 64*) whose males make shrill sounds by vibrating tiny membranes at the sides of their bodies. Well camouflaged as they suck sap from the branches of trees and shrubs, they fly rapidly when disturbed. The nymphs spend several years feeding on roots and then climb the stems where the adults – often pale green at first – break out of their skins.

1 *Cicada orni*, often covered with waxy grey powder, has 11 small spots on each shiny forewing. It lives in southern Europe.

2 *Cicadetta montana* is the only British cicada and is very rare here. Its soft, warbling song is not easy to hear. Several similar species live in southern Europe.

3 Centrotus cornutus belongs to a group of homopterans known as treehoppers. The pronotum (*see Introduction*) extends right to the back of the body in the form of an arched spine. It feeds on a wide range of plants, mainly in woodlands.

4 Epiptera europaea is easily recognised by its strongly pointed head and its clear network of veins. It feeds on many kinds of plants in southern and central Europe, but does not occur in Britain.

5 Buffalo Hopper (*Stictocephalus bisonia*) is an American treehopper now well established in southern Europe and feeding on many kinds of plants. Notice how the horned thorax overhangs the head.

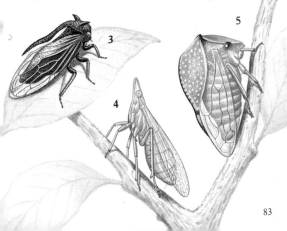

FROGHOPPERS

Froghoppers are homopteran bugs which get their name from their leaping abilities and the vaguely frog-like appearance of some of the species. The hind legs have just two stout spines, which distinguish them from the leafhoppers (*see pages 86-7*). they are also known as spittle bugs because the nymphs live in a mass of froth which they pump out from their hind ends. This prevents them from drying up and also protects them from enemies.

1 *Cercopis vulnerata* is common on vegetation in summer in ′southern and central Europe. Its bright colours indicate that it has a nasty taste. The nymphs live underground in a mass of solidified froth, sucking sap from roots. Several similar species live on the continent.

1

2

x 4

x 4

2 *Aphrophora alni* can be found on many trees and shrubs. It is one of several species with a distinct ridge or keel on the front half of the pronotum and is much larger than the next species.

3 Common Froghopper (*Philaenus spumarius*) is the most familiar of our froghoppers, although its wing patterns vary a good deal. The nymphal froth (**3a**) is abundant on vegetation in late spring and is commonly called cuckoo-spit. Look inside it to see the nymph (**3b**).

4 *Cixius nervosus*, only distantly related to the froghoppers, has much straighter margins to its wings. Notice the prominent veins. It lives mainly on trees.

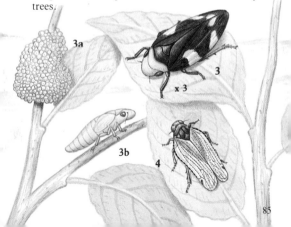

3a

3

x 3

3b

4

LEAFHOPPERS

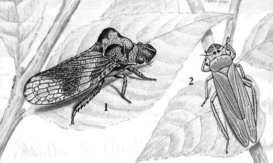

Leafhoppers are a large group of homopterans, often very colourful, although the individual insects are generally very small. The forewings are usually rather tough, and the hind legs bear numerous small spines. Many are pests, especially in tropical regions. They jump well and most also fly well.

1 *Ledra aurita* is easily recognised by its unusual shape. There is nothing else like it in Europe. Notice the 'ears' on the thorax. It feeds mainly on oak and is hard to spot at rest on the branches.

2 *Cicadella viridis* is common on grasses and other low-growing vegetation, especially in damp places, throughout the summer. Male forewings may be brown or purplish.

3 Zygina flammigera sometimes lacks the red band on its head, and that on the thorax may be divided down the centre. It lives on various trees and shrubs and, unlike most leafhoppers, passes the winter as an adult – usually hiding in evergreens.

4 Graphocephala fennahi is a North American leafhopper, introduced to Britain and now found quite commonly on wild and cultivated rhododendrons in the southern half of the country.

5 Eupteryx aurata is abundant on many low-growing plants, especially nettles, from spring until late autumn. It often swarms over potatoes, its feeding punctures producing small pale spots on the leaves.

87

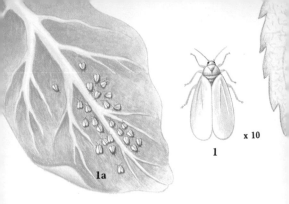

x 10

1

1a

WHITEFLIES & PSYLLIDS

The whiteflies are very small homopteran bugs whose wings are clothed with waxy white powder. They look very like tiny moths. Look for them on the undersides of leaves. Like the aphids (*see page 90*) the whiteflies exude lots of honeydew which makes the plant leaves very sticky.

1 Cabbage Whitefly (*Aleyrodes proletella*) is often very common on cabbages and related plants. Large clusters may sit sucking sap from the undersides of the leaves (**1a**) and they fly up in clouds if you disturb them. The Greenhouse Whitefly is very similar. Look for it on tomatoes, cucumbers and other plants in the greenhouse or indoors. When they are very numerous they weaken the plants by taking too much sap.

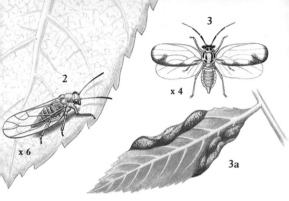

Psyllids are a large group of leaping homopterans, also known as jumping plant lice. They resemble leafhoppers, but with antennae much longer than the tiny bristle-like antennae of the hoppers. The wing veins all appear to come from a central stalk. Most species are associated with just one kind of plant.

2 Apple Sucker (*Psylla mali*) is abundant on apple trees. Bright green in spring and summer, it turns reddish brown in autumn. It passes the winter in the egg stage and the flat, red-eyed nymphs feed on the flower buds in spring.

3 Ash Psyllid (*Psyllopsis fraxini*) is responsible for deforming ash leaves (**3a**). If you open one of these crinkled leaves, which generally have prominent red veins, you will find numerous nymphs.

APHIDS

Blackfly, greenfly and blight are common names for aphids – pear-shaped little homopterans which can be such a nuisance in the garden. They weaken plants by taking large amounts of sap and by spreading virus diseases. Much of the sugar taken in with the sap is passed out as sticky honeydew, which often attracts ants. There are winged and wingless individuals in each species. For much of the year the females give birth to babies without mating.

1 Black Bean Aphid (*Aphis fabae*) smothers beans and many other plants in summer (**1a**). All are females at this time and each can have several babies in a day. The colonies grow quickly and the winged aphids fly to fresh plants. Males appear in autumn and, after mating, the females lay eggs on spindle and some other shrubs. The eggs hatch in spring and the aphids gradually move to the summer host plants.

2 *Macrosiphum rosae* is the usual greenfly on roses in spring. It may be green or pink. It moves to scabious and teasel for the summer and then returns to lay winter eggs on the roses.

3 Cabbage Aphid (*Brevicoryne brassicae*) forms dense, mealy colonies on brassicas (**3a**). It lays eggs on the same plants in autumn, but in mild years the females can go on giving birth all winter.

4 Woolly Aphid (*Eriosoma lanigerum*) forms fluffy clusters on apple branches in spring and summer (**4a**). An alien from North America, no males are known in Europe and females bear live young.

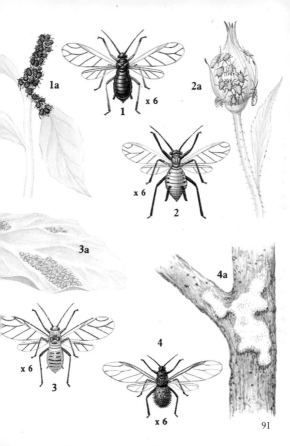

1a

1 x 6

2a

x 6 2

3a

x 6 3

4

4a

x 6

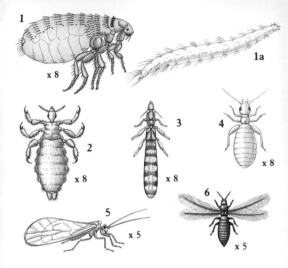

FLEAS, LICE & OTHERS

1 Cat Flea (*Ctenocephalides felis*) is the commonest household flea, often living on pet cats in large numbers and commonly biting people as well. The larva (**1a**) lives in the cats' sleeping quarters, feeding on assorted debris and the droppings of the adult fleas from which it gets a certain amount of partly digested blood. There are many different kinds of fleas – all feeding on the blood of birds and mammals – but you need a microscope to identify them properly.

2 Human Louse (*Pediculus humanus*) is generally found on the head, gripping the hair with its strong claws. It sucks blood and can transmit several diseases. Apart from size, adults and nymphs look much alike. Athough much less common than it used to be, the louse occasionally builds up large populations – especially in school children.

3 Feather Louse (*Columbicola claviformis*) is one of many biting lice that infest birds. Instead of sucking blood, like the human louse, it chews skin and feathers. Many related lice are shorter and fatter. Look for them on any dead birds.

4 Booklouse (*Liposcelis terricolis*) is one of several similar wingless scavengers in the house. Notice the broad hind legs. Feeding on both plant and animal matter, these insects often damage books. They belong to a large group known as psocids.

5 *Stenopsocus immaculatus* is one of many rather similar winged psocids feeding on algae and pollen grains on trees and shrubs. It is like a psyllid (*see page 89*) but has no beak.

6 Cereal Thrips (*Limothrips cerealium*) develops in cereal ears. Great swarms fly off in summer and often hibernate in houses. They are often called thunder bugs, because they tend to fly in thundery weather. Many similar species can be found in flowers, piercing the petals and sucking out sap.

SCORPION, SNAKE & ALDER FLIES

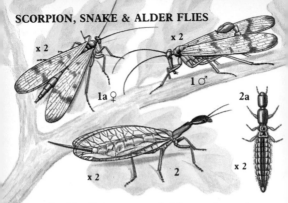

1 Scorpion Fly (*Panorpa germanica*) is one of several similar species named because the tail end of males turns up like that of a scorpion, although it is completely harmless. Female (**1a**) has a straight abdomen. Scorpion flies are scavengers, feeding on rotting fruit, dead insects and even bird droppings. They like shady places and are weak fliers. Larvae (**1b**) live in the soil.

2 Snake Fly (*Raphidia maculicollis*) gets its name for its long neck. There are several similar species, differing mainly in the shape of the head and the arrangement of the wing veins. They live mainly in wooded areas, where females use their long ovipositor to lay eggs in bark crevices of dead and decaying trees. Larvae (**2a**) feed on beetle grubs in the timber.

3 Alder Fly (*Sialis lutaria*) is related to both the Snake fly and the lacewings (*see page 96-7*). Larvae (**3a**) live in still and slow-moving water and feed on various other creatures. Adults emerge in late spring and early summer, flying weakly and usually to be found sitting on waterside vegetation. They feed but rarely – perhaps nibbling a few pollen grains – and lay their eggs in large batches (**3b**) on plants overhanging the water. Larvae simply fall in when they hatch. A similar, but darker species, *S. fuliginosa*, breeds only in running water.

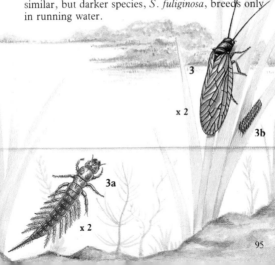

3

x 2

x 2

3b

3a

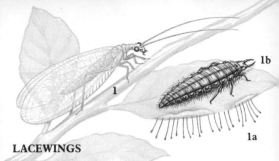

LACEWINGS

Lacewings are delicate green or brown insects with rather weak flight. They are named for the lacy network of veins on the wings. They are mainly nocturnal, although you will often disturb them on vegetation by day, and they commonly come to lighted windows in the evening. There are many species and they all feed on aphids. The green lacewings and some of the larger brown species lay their eggs at the tips of delicate threads formed from quick-setting gum which they secrete (**1a**). Larvae (**1b**) also feed on aphids, sucking them dry with the aid of curved, hollow jaws. Some species camouflage themselves with the empty aphid skins.

1 *Chrysopa septempunctata* is bright green and has seven *small* black spots on its face. It is common in woods, gardens and hedgerows.

2 *Chrysopa perla* is distinctly bluish-green with plenty of black on the wing veins and the body. It lives mainly in wooded habitats.

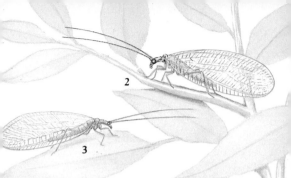

3 *Chrysopa carnea* is common everywhere and, unlike most lacewings, it hibernates as an adult – often in houses. It is bright green in spring and summer, but becomes flesh-coloured, as shown, during hibernation.

4 *Hemerobius humulinus* is one of several very similar brown lacewings living mainly in wooded areas. Its larva (**4a**) is less bristly than those of the green lacewings.

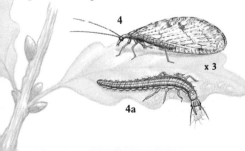

x 3

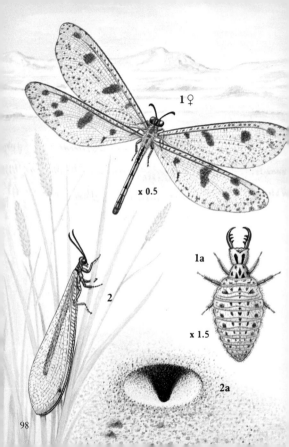

1 ♀

x 0.5

2

1a

x 1.5

2a

ANT-LIONS

Ant-lions are close relatives of the lacewings, although they are generally much larger. They look more like dragonflies (*see page 22-9*) or damselflies (*see page 30-7*) but they have much larger antennae. Males have prominent claspers at the rear. Flight is slow and fluttery. The insects are mostly nocturnal, although some fly by day, and they pluck small insects from the vegetation. They get their name because their larvae (**1a**) are fierce predators of ants and other ground-living insects. Some dig pits in which to trap their prey (**2a**). There are no ant-lions in Britain, but several live on the continent – mainly in the south.

1 *Palpares libelluloides* is Europe's largest ant-lion, flying weakly in the sunshine around the Mediterranean. Like all ant-lions, it favours dry sandy habitats. Larva (**1a**) rests in the sand, with just the tips of its huge jaws showing, and rushes out to attack anything that passes by. It grabs all kinds of insects and pulls them down into the sand to suck them dry.

2 *Myrmeleon formicarius* is *the* ant-lion, found nearly all over Europe including southern Scandinavia. Adult are difficult to spot when resting on the vegetation by day. Larva uses its jaws to dig a conical pit in the sand (**2a**) and buries itself at the bottom with just the jaws showing. When ants and other prey stumble into the pit the loose sand prevents them from scrambling out again, and the larva may actually throw sand at them with its jaws. When they finally fall to the bottom they are eagerly snapped up.

ASCALAPHIDS & MANTIS FLY

Ascalaphids are related to the ant-lions of the previous page but have much longer antennae and fly much more rapidly. Active mainly in sunshine, they hawk to and fro – generally over rough grassland – and snatch small insects in flight. Only the males have the prominent claspers at the rear. In dull weather they rest with their wings held tent-like over the body (**1a**). Larvae are like those of the ant-lions but live in leaf litter and other debris and never make pits. None lives in Britain or northern Europe.

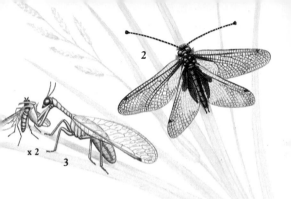

x 2

2

3

1 *Libelloides longicornis* has yellow veins in the dark areas at the base of the forewings. It flies in southern parts of Europe to the west of the Alps.

2 *Libelloides coccajus* is more widespread than the previous species and has a larger black patch on the hind wing. The pale areas may be white or yellow.

3 Mantis Fly (*Mantispa styriaca*) looks and behaves like a small mantis (*see page 58*), but its flimsy, net-veined wings show that it is more closely related to the lacewings. It feeds on small flies which it plucks from the vegetation. It flies well by day and by night, mainly in lightly wooded and scrubby areas. Larvae grow up as parasites in the egg cocoons of various spiders. The mantis fly lives mainly in southern Europe and is not found in Britain.

CADDIS FLIES

Caddis flies are often mistaken for moths, but if you look carefully – preferably with a lens – you will see that their wings are clothed with minute hairs instead of the scales found in moths. And caddis flies never have the tubular tongue or proboscis found in most moths. Some may nibble pollen grains, but most do not feed in the adult state. They always rest with the wings held tent-like over the body and the antennae pointing forwards. Nearly 200 species live in Britain, with many more on the continent. Most are brown or black. Look for the stout spurs on the legs to help with identification. Caddis flies grow up in fresh water. They often come to lights at night. Some larvae live freely on the bottom of the pond or stream, while others spin little nets which trap food particles in the water. Best known, however, are those that make portable cases with sand grains or plant fragments. Several of these cases are shown on page 105.

1 _Phryganea grandis_ is Europe's largest caddis fly, recognised by the wing pattern. There are two spurs

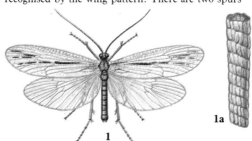

1a

1

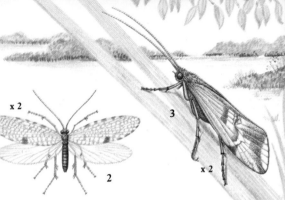

on the front leg and four on each of the others. It breeds in still waters where larvae make cases of spirally arranged plant fragments. (**1a**)

2 _Philopotamus montanus_ has the same spur count as the last species. It breeds mainly in upland streams, where larvae are net-spinners.

3 _Limnephilus lunatus_ is one of many rather similar species with clear patches in the forewings and with very clear hind wings. They are never very hairy. Notice the sharply truncated wings with the pale crescent, typical of this species, at the tip. Spur count: 1 on the front leg, 3 on the middle and 4 on the hind leg. They breed in any kind of water. Larval case is made of overlapping leaf fragments and other debris.

1 Ceraclea nigronervosa has two spurs on each leg. Notice the prominent wing veins. It is a strong flier, breeding in lakes and large rivers of northern and central Europe. Larval case is made of silk with irregular bands of sand.

2 Mystacides azurea has no spurs on the front legs and two on each of the others. Notice the very long antennae. It is sometimes known as the silverhorn. It breeds in still water and the larval case is a tapering tube of sand grains.

Each case-building species has its own building plan and some of the many varieties are shown opposite. *Triaenodes* actually swims in its case by rowing with its long middle legs. *Odontocerum* has a typical case, open at both ends. *Agapetus* cases are permanently fixed to stones on the stream bed. Mature *Brachycentrus* cases consist only of silk and are fixed to plants. The small twigs attached to the *Anabolia* case may protect it from trout and other fishes. The *Molanna* case, seen here from below, has a broad protective shield over the top. The insects pupate in their cases and, when ready, the pupae swim to the surface to release the adults. The latter often swarm over the water in large numbers in the evening.

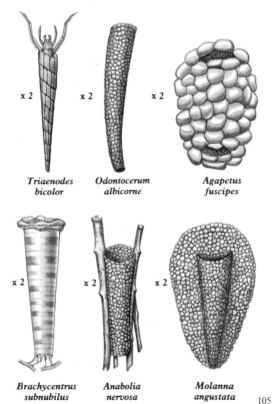

Triaenodes bicolor

Odontocerum albicorne

Agapetus fuscipes

Brachycentrus subnubilus

Anabolia nervosa

Molanna angustata

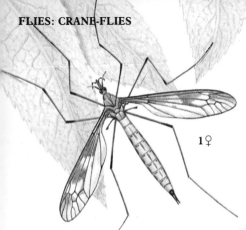

1 ♀

The true flies, unlike almost all other flying insects, have only two wings. The hind pair have been much modified during evolution and are now represented by a pair of tiny pin-like organs called halteres – well seen in the crane-flies pictured here, but covered by flaps in most of the bulkier flies.

1 *Tipula maxima* is Britain's largest fly, always resting with wings outstretched. Adults rarely feed, although they occasionally lap up nectar. Larvae live in mud at the edges of ponds and streams. Like the other flies on this page, it belongs to the group known as crane-flies. The V-shaped groove on the thorax is typical of the whole group.

2 Tipula paludosa is abundant on farmland and often in the garden as well. Male has a swollen tip to his abdomen (**2a**). Female uses her pointed abdomen to lay eggs in the soil, where the larva – the infamous leatherjacket (**2b**) – feeds on roots. It may also chew through stems at the soil surface. *Tipula oleracea* is very similar and equally common, but the female wings are as long as the abdomen: in *paludosa* they are slightly shorter.

3 Nephrotoma appendiculata rests with its wings folded flat over the body. It is abundant in gardens, where larvae – just like those of *paludosa* – cause much damage to roots.

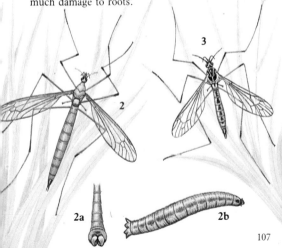

FLIES: MOSQUITOES

The mosquitoes are slender flies whose females all suck blood from birds and mammals. They also take nectar, but without blood they cannot produce their eggs. Males, recognised by their very feathery antennae (**3a**), which pick up the high-pitched humming sounds of the females, feed entirely on nectar. Both sexes have a long, hollow proboscis with which they suck up food. The wing veins are clothed with scales. Larvae and pupae live in water and pupae (**3c**) are very mobile, although they do not feed. Larvae feed on minute plants and animals.

1 Anopheles maculipennis, like other members of its genus, has long palps in both sexes, those of males being like tiny golf clubs. The abdomen lacks scales and the insect rests with its body steeply inclined to the surface on which it rests (**1a**). Females can carry

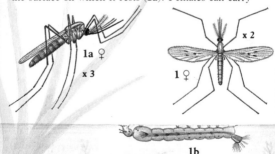

malaria. Larva (**1b**) rests horizontally at water surface but wriggles rapidly away when disturbed.

2 Aedes cantans rests, like the next species, with the body arched and the abdomen more or less parallel to the surface. The abdomen bears scales. Male palps are long and ornately feathered: female palps are short. It lives in shady places, where a female will bite us readily. There are several similar species.

3 Culex pipiens is very common but does not normally bite us: it prefers birds. The abdomen is scaled and rather blunt at the tip. Female palps are short but those of males are very long (**3a**). It breeds in all kinds of still water, including garden ponds and water butts. Larva (**3b**) at rest hangs from the water surface. Pupa (**3c**) has almost straight abdomen: *Anopheles* pupa is strongly curved.

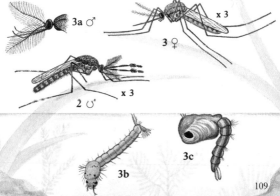

3a ♂

x 3

3 ♀

x 3

2 ♂

3c

3b

FLIES contd.

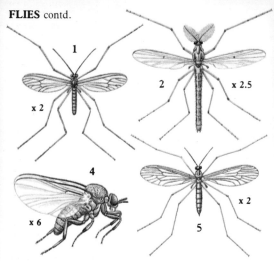

1 *Dixella aestivalis* is one of several very similar flies, related to mosquitoes but without scales on the veins. Male antennae are not feathery and females do not suck blood. Adults swarm over water throughout the year. U-shaped larvae float in surface layers, feeding on minute plants and animals.

2 *Chironomus plumosus* resembles the mosquito in having plumed antennae in the male, but the wings are not scaled and the veins are very weak. The wings are held tent-like over the body at rest, always leaving the tip of the abdomen exposed. Larvae (**2a**), known as bloodworms, live in tubes of mud in stagnant water. There are many similar species, none of them blood-suckers.

3 Phantom Larva (*Chaoborus crystallinus*) is the colourless larva of a fly related to mosquitoes but not blood-sucking and with scales only on the wing margins. Look for it in ponds throughout the year.

4 Black-fly (*Simulium equinum*) is one of many very similar dark, hunch-backed flies with broad wings. Females suck blood and, existing in vast numbers, can make life very unpleasant for us around upland streams. Larvae (**4a**) live under stones in running water.

5 *Trichocera annulata* is one of a group known as winter gnats, because they are most common in winter. They often swarm in the garden in the afternoon. The short, sharply curved vein at the rear of the wing, distinguishes the winter gnats from small crane-flies. Larvae live in rotting vegetation.

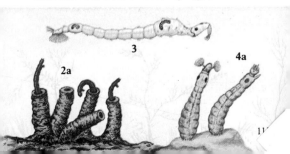

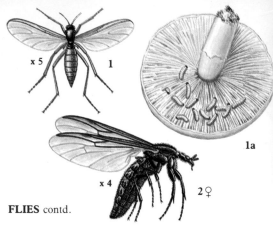

FLIES contd.

1 *Sciara thomae* is one of a whole army of small flies called fungus gnats: their larvae (**1a**) feed largely on fungi and several species cause damage to cultivated mushrooms. They also breed in garden compost heaps, from where the adult *Sciara* often enters houses. It commonly scuttles away when disturbed.

2 St Mark's-fly (*Bibio marci*) is named because it is often abundant around St Mark's Day (April 25th). You will find males swarming over farmland, especially near trees, drifting slowly through the air with their long legs trailing. Females are more likely to be found sitting on the vegetation. Male head is much larger than that of female. The fly is also

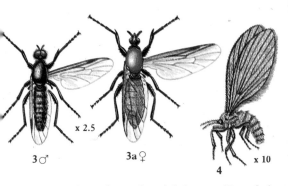

x 2.5

3♂　　　**3a♀**　　　**4**　　　**x 10**

common in gardens, where it helps to pollinate fruit trees. Larvae feed on roots and decaying vegetable matter in the soil.

3 Bibio hortulanus has habits similar to those of the last species, but the sexes differ markedly in colour. The female (**3a**) has a much narrower head and smaller eyes. The fly is very common in gardens. A stout spur on the front leg distinguishes *Bibio* species from the very similar fever-fly (*Dilophus febrilis*), which has a small circlet of spines.

4 Psychoda is a genus of very small, hairy flies known as moth-flies or owl midges. The species are very difficult to separate. They breed in damp and decaying matter and are abundant at sewage works. They fly mainly in damp weather, often coming to lighted windows in the evening.

FLIES contd.

1 Stratiomys potamida belongs to the group known as soldier-flies: many of the species have bright colours reminiscent of military uniforms. It occurs in marshy habitats but is not common. Larva is carnivorous and aquatic. Notice the characteristic venation of the group, with rather weak veins towards the rear of the wings.

2 Chloromyia formosa is another soldier-fly, recognised by its colour and its very hairy eyes. Female abdomen has browner hairs, with a violet sheen showing through them. Fond of sunbathing on leaves, it is common in the garden. Larva feeds on decaying matter, often in the compost heap.

3 Bee-fly (*Bombylius major*) is very well named, for it is just like a bumblebee when feeding at flowers (**3a**). Although its wings continue to beat, the front legs grip the flower while the fly plunges its long, rigid

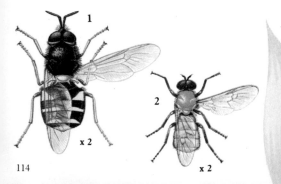

1

2

x 2

x 2

beak in to reach the nectar. It is quite harmless. A sun-loving and extremely agile insect, it is abundant in flowery places, including gardens, in the spring. Female scatters her eggs while hovering close to the ground and larvae make their way to the nests of various mining bees (*pages 164-5*) where they feed on the bee grubs and their stored food.

4 *Thyridanthrax fenestratus* is related to the bee-fly, although it lacks a long proboscis. It inhabits sandy places, where larvae parasitise various caterpillars. Several species occur in southern Europe.

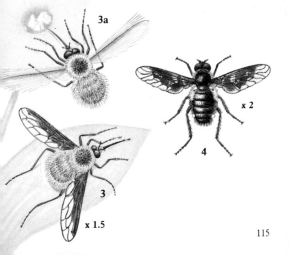

3a

3

x 1.5

x 2

4

HORSE-FLIES

The horse-flies are stout-bodied insects, often with beautifully coloured eyes in life. They are generally fast and agile through the air and active mainly in the sunshine. The wing-veins form a broad V across the wing-tip. Females are voracious blood-suckers, attacking all kinds of large mammals, including us. Males feed on nectar. Larvae live mainly in damp soil, feeding on both decaying matter and small animals.

1 Tabanus sudeticus varies in colour but generally has *distinct* pale triangles on the abdomen – usually confined to the rear half of each segment. Living on pastures and in open woodland, it is mainly an upland species in Britain.

2 Tabanus bromius ranges from fawn or grey to black, generally with one dark horizontal band across each eye. It is the commonest of several similar species on the pastures of Europe.

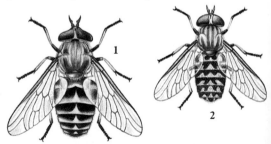

3 x 2

3 *Chrysops relictus* is one of several rather similar species with beautifully patterned eyes. Male usually has more extensive black markings on wings than female. It lives mostly on damp heaths and in light woodland.

4 Cleg-fly (*Haematopota pluvialis*) is one of Europe's commonest horse-flies, especially in damp woods and other poorly-drained areas. Particularly active in overcast conditions, its silent flight means that it often bites – painfully – before you notice it. There are several similar species.

4 x 3

ROBBER-FLIES

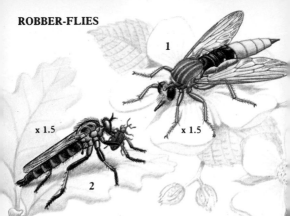

Robber-flies are mostly sturdily built flies that capture other insects, usually in mid-air, with the aid of bristly legs. They usually rest on the ground or prominent perches and dart out when possible prey comes within range. The prey is then sucked dry with the stout, forward-pointing proboscis. There is a deep groove between the eyes in both sexes (the eyes are touching in most other male flies) and strong bristles on the face protect the eyes from the struggling prey. Most species are rather drab, with a tapering abdomen. Larvae feed mainly in rotting vegetation.

1 *Asilus crabroniformis* is an unmistakable species of heathland and other open country. It breeds in cow pats and other dung.

2 *Neoitamus cyanurus* occurs mainly in oakwoods. Male has a steely blue patch just before the tip of the abdomen. Female has a shiny black, telescopic ovipositor which she uses to lay her eggs in the buds of trees and shrubs, although resulting larvae fall to feed on the woodland floor.

3 *Dioctria rufipes* is less hairy than most robber flies, with antennae springing from a bulge on the top of the head. Front and middle femora are yellow and hind femora are black, a combination which distinguishes this species from several similar ones. It lives mainly in wooded areas.

4 *Laphria gibbosa* is a striking robber-fly preying partly on the bumblebees which it so closely resembles. Larvae live in decaying wood. It is not found in Britain.

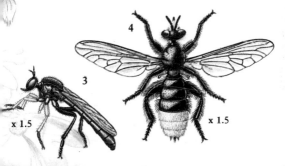

FLIES contd.

1 *Empis tessellata* preys on other flies which it catches on various flowers. It is especially fond of hunting on hawthorn blossom and umbellifer heads. Notice the stout beak used to drain the prey's juices and also to suck nectar. Larvae are predatory and live mainly in leaf litter.

2 Snipe-fly (*Rhagio scolopacea*) is most often seen sitting in a head-down position on trees and walls. Its pattern varies but the thorax is always grey with yellow 'shoulders'. Larvae prey on small creatures in leaf litter and rotting wood.

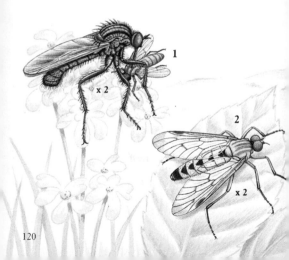

3 *Conops quadrifasciatus* is an excellent wasp mimic (*see Introduction*). Look for it on umbellifer heads, where it likes to sunbathe in spring and summer. Adult takes nectar, but larvae are internal parasites of bumblebees. Eggs are laid on the bees in flight and carried to the nest, where the resulting grubs burrow into the bee larvae.

4 *Poecilobothrus nobilitatus* lives around the edges of ponds, settling on stones and vegetation with the front end of the body raised, in a pose characteristic of this and many related species. Male has white wing tips. It feeds on other small animals. The mud-dwelling larvae are also carnivorous.

3

x 3

x 3   4 ♀

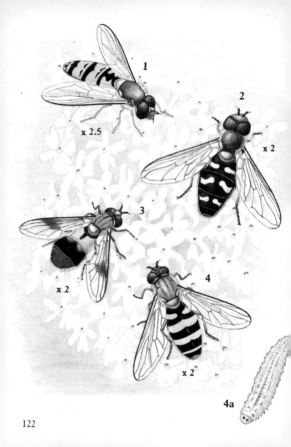

1

x 2.5

2

x 2

3

x 2

4

x 2

4a

HOVER-FLIES

The hover-flies form a very large and varied group, generally recognised by the false margin, just inside the outer edge of the wing. It is formed by the forward-curving and linking of some of the veins. The insects possess remarkable hovering abilities, hanging on the air in shafts of sunlight, darting away when disturbed but soon returning to the same spot. Many mimic bees and wasps and thereby fool many birds, although their antennae are quite different and they have only one pair of wings. They feed on nectar and some also crush and ingest pollen grains. They are particularly fond of umbellifer flowers, where the nectar is freely accessible to their short tongues. Larval habits are varied: many prey on aphids, some live in dung and other decaying matter, a few attack living plants, and some even live as scavengers in the nests of bees and wasps.

1 *Episyrphus balteatus*, recognised by the thin black stripes on its abdomen, often migrates in large swarms. It is abundant in gardens.

2 *Scaeva pyrastri* is another common garden species, easily recognised by its cream or white patches.

3 *Leucozona lucorum* is distinguished by the pale area at the front of the abdomen. *Volucella pellucens* has a similar pattern but is larger and the first two long wing veins join before reaching the wing-tip.

4 *Syrphus ribesii* often swarms on umbellifer heads. Like those of the other hover-flies on this page, its larvae (**4a**) eat aphids.

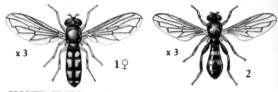

x 3

x 3

1 ♀

2

HOVER-FLIES contd.

1 *Melanostoma scalare* has a parallel-sided abdomen, slimmer in male than in female. Very fond of hawthorn blossom in spring, it can be found on most garden and hedgerow flowers from spring until late autumn. The wings are generally folded flat over the abdomen when feeding. Other hover-flies can do this, but many prefer to keep their wings at least slightly spread. Larvae eat aphids.

2 *Neoascia podagrica* is another very common garden hover-fly, distinguished from several similar species by the clouding on the outer cross-veins. There is no obvious false margin. Larva eats aphids.

3 Narcissus-fly (*Merodon equestris*) is one of the less welcome garden species, for its larva feeds in and destroys the bulbs of narcissi and related plants (**3b**). Two of the several colour forms are shown here. They mimic several species of bumblebees. Like many other species, they emit a high-pitched whine when hovering, but they spend much of their time sunbathing on the ground or low-growing plants. Notice the deep curve in the third long vein.

4 *Volucella bombylans* is another variable species mimicking several kinds of bumblebees. Some specimens are almost completely black. The first two long veins meet before reaching the wing-tip, the third long vein is almost straight. Larvae live in bee and wasp nests, feeding partly on the droppings of the grubs. Several close relatives, all with similar wing venation, are black and yellow mimics of wasps.

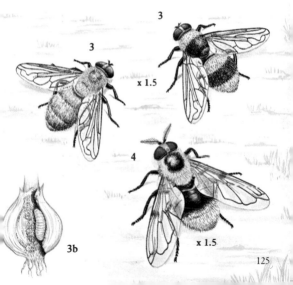

3

3

x 1.5

4

3b

x 1.5

HOVER-FLIES contd.

1 *Chrysotoxum cautum* is one of several similar species with long, forward-pointing antennae. Look for it in woods, hedgerows and gardens where it likes to sunbathe on leaves. Larvae feed in rotting wood. Southern and central Europe.

2 *Helophilus pendulus* frequents waterside vegetation. Males often hover just above the water. Notice the deep curve in the third long vein. Larva is like that of the next species and lives in muddy water.

3 Drone-fly (*Eristalis tenax*) gets its name from its uncanny likeness to a male honey bee (*page 169*). The pale spots at the front of the abdomen range from cream to yellowish brown and are sometimes absent. The first two long veins join before reaching the

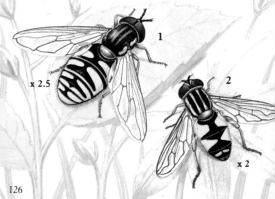

x 2.5

x 2

wing margin. Adults may be seen sunning themselves on walls even in the middle of winter and they are among the first insects to visit the snowdrops and other spring flowers. There are several similar species, distinguished partly by the colours of their legs. Larva (**3a**) is known as the rat-tailed maggot. It lives in stagnant water, including blocked house gutters, and breathes by pushing its telescopic tail up to the surface.

4 *Rhingia campestris*, easily identified by its snout, frequents fields and hedgerows. Larva feeds in cow pats.

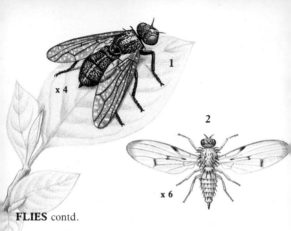

FLIES contd.

1 *Platystoma seminationis* is a rather lethargic fly, most likely to be found crawling on vegetation in shady places. The underside of the abdomen is pale cream. Larvae feed in decaying vegetation, including garden compost heaps.

2 *Palloptera arcuata* can be recognisd by its colour and the light spotting of the wings. Female has a non-retractable ovipositor sheath. It is common on low-growing vegetation, especially in damp or shady places, throughout the summer. It often waves its wings as it walks. Larvae feed in decaying vegetable matter. Several related species have darker or more extensive wing markings.

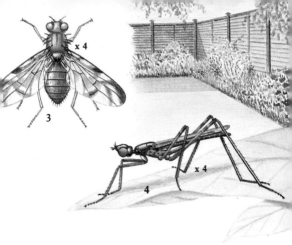

3 Celery-fly (*Euleia heraclei*) has dark brown or reddish markings on wings and body. Larva lives inside the leaves of hogweed and other umbellifers, including garden celery and parsnips, where it makes yellowish brown blotches throughout the summer.

4 *Micropeza corrigiolata* is one of the stilt-legged flies, so called for their very long legs. Look for it crawling slowly over shady vegetation. It is not uncommon on garden shrubs. Larvae live in rotting vegetation. A close relative (*M. lateralis*) is much more yellow, and there are also completely black species on the continent.

1 ***Sepsis fulgens*** is one of several very similar small flies with a prominent spot near the wing-tip. They wave their wings slowly up and down as they sit on or walk over low-growing vegetation, especially along hedgerows and woodland margins. They hibernate as adults, often forming dense swarms on the vegetation (**1a**) before entering their winter quarters. Larvae feed in dung.

2 ***Phytomyza ilicis*** s well known for the mines which its larvae make in holly leaves (**2a**), but adults are rarely noticed. There are many similar species, all lacking a cross vein in the outer part of the wing. You can obtain adults from mined leaves collected in early

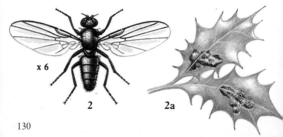

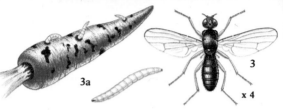

summer: a small hole in the mine surface indicates that the fly has already flown.

3 Carrot-fly (*Psila rosae*) is one of several similar species with a distinct break about a quarter of the way along the front margin of the wing. Its larvae cause serious damage to carrot roots (**3a**), infested plants often being recognised in the garden by their reddish leaves.

4 *Drosophila funebris* is one of a group of tiny flies known as fruit-flies. They are very fond of ripe fruit and all kinds of fermenting materials and are sometimes a nuisance in jam factories and canneries and wherever beer and wine are to be found. Wine corks attract them in the summer (**4a**).

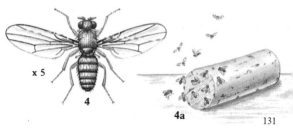

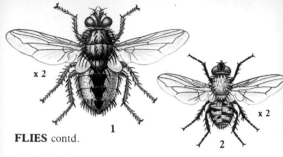

x 2

1

x 2

2

FLIES contd.

1 *Tachina fera* is one of a large group of rather bristly flies whose larvae live as parasites inside the caterpillars of butterflies and moths. It is particularly common on waterside plants in late summer, laying its eggs on the plants from where the grubs bore into their caterpillar hosts.

2 Cluster-fly (*Pollenia rudis*), recognised by its abdominal pattern and golden thoracic hairs, is so named because it gathers in large numbers to hibernate in attics and out-buildings. Larvae live parasitically inside earthworms.

3 *Lucilia caesar* is a common blow-fly, usually known as a greenbottle because of its colour. The sharply bent fourth long vein combines with silvery jowls below the eyes to distinguish *Lucilia* species from several other metallic green flies. The life history is like that of *Calliphora*, but *Lucilia* rarely enters houses.

4 Flesh-fly (*Sarcophaga carnaria*) is one of several red-eyed species with very large feet. It varies a good deal in size. It breeds in carrion and may investigate your dustbin, although it rarely enters the house. Female brings forth small larvae instead of laying eggs.

5 *Calliphora vomitoria* is one of our commonest bluebottles or blow-flies, laying its eggs on our meat and fish and on assorted carrion in the wild. Larvae (**5a**) feed on the liquefying flesh and soon turn into barrel-shaped pupae (**5b**). Adults can be found throughout the year often basking on walls in the winter sunshine. Like the other flies shown here, they feed by mopping up liquids with a sponge-like tongue.

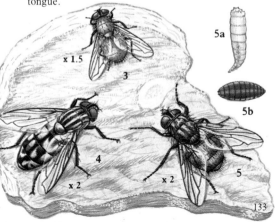

x 1.5

3

5a

5b

4

x 2

5

x 2

FLIES contd.

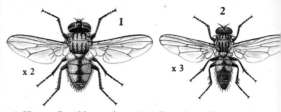

1 House-fly (*Musca domestica*) lives in and around houses all over the world. It is especially common near farms and rubbish dumps, where it breeds in all kinds of manure and other decaying matter. Larva is like that of the bluebottle (*page 132*). Adult uses its mop-like tongue to feed on almost anything, but is especially fond of sweet things and decaying matter: solid food is dealt with by pouring saliva over it and sucking up the resulting solution. Like the bluebottle it carries many germs from the rubbish to our food.

2 Lesser House-fly (*Fannia canicularis*) resembles a small house-fly but its fourth long vein is almost

134

straight instead of sharply bent. Males fly incessantly round lamp-shades in our houses by day.

3 *Mesembrina meridiana* occurs mainly in hedge-rows and wooded areas, where it feeds on nectar. Larva lives in dung.

4 Yellow Dung-fly (*Scathophaga stercoraria*) swarms all over cow pats and horse dung, flying up in clouds when disturbed. Female is greyer and less furry. Adults catch other small flies, while larvae feed in the dung.

5 Deer-fly (*Lipoptena cervi*) feeds on the blood of deer, mainly in wooded areas. Female gives birth periodically to a fully grown larva, which pupates in the ground. New adults fly into the trees and drop on to passing animals - including us! On reaching a suitable host, the insects shed their wings.

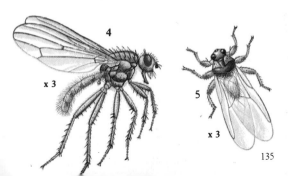

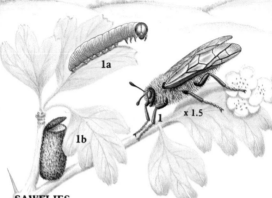

SAWFLIES

The sawflies get their name from the tiny, saw-like ovipositor of most females. It is used for slitting plants, the eggs being laid in the slits. Not true flies, these insects belong to the same order as the bees and wasps, but have no narrow waist and no sting. Adults are active mainly by day, feeding largely on pollen, although some are partly carnivorous. Larvae are vegetarian, generally like the caterpillars of butterflies and moths but easily distinguished by having more than five pairs of fleshy legs in addition to the three pairs of true legs at the front.

1 Hawthorn Sawfly (*Trichiosoma tibiale*) is a fast-flying, bee-like species. Larva (**1a**) feeds on hawthorn

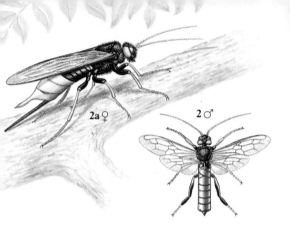

2a ♀

2 ♂

but, despite its size, is rarely noticed. Much more obvious is the sausage-shaped cocoon (**1b**) which remains glued to the bare twigs through the winter. Adult cuts its way out in spring, making quite a noise as it uses its jaws to slice around the top like a tin-opener.

2 Horntail (*Urocerus gigas*) is also known as the wood wasp, although it is quite harmless despite the female's awesome ovipositor (**2a**). She uses this like a drill instead of a saw and lays her eggs in pine trunks. Larvae are virtually legless and feed on the timber. Although found mainly in woodlands, the insects often emerge from wood stacked in timber yards.

SAWFLIES contd.

1 *Acantholyda erythrocephala* is a fast-flying, sun-loving insect of open pine woods. Male head is largely black. Larvae live communally in webs on pines, sometimes causing severe damage. In Britain it is found mainly in the north.

2 *Abia sericea*, closely related to the hawthorn sawfly (*page 136*), is a fast-flying species of sunny grasslands. Adults can be found on flowers throughout the summer. Female has a purplish thorax. Larva feeds on scabious.

3 *Pontania proxima* is responsible for the bean galls that develop on the leaves of crack and white willow (**3a**). The galls are often paler on white willow. Female lays her eggs in the leaves and a gall swells up around each egg. The resulting grub gradually hollows out the gall and emerges to pupate in the soil or in a bark crevice when mature. Most adults are female and they lay eggs without mating. There are

x 2 3 3a

several similar species, causing galls on various kinds of sallow.

4 Gooseberry Sawfly (*Nematus ribesii*) is abundant in gardens, where its larvae (**4a**) feed avidly on gooseberry and currant leaves. Male is much smaller and mainly black. There are many similar species.

5 *Croesus septentrionalis* is best known for its larvae, which strip the leaves from birches and other small trees. They live in colonies and when alarmed they raise their hind ends and release a pungent smell which deters most of their enemies. Adults are about 10mm long, with a red band on the abdomen and conspicuously swollen hind feet.

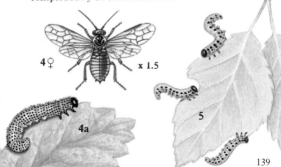

4 ♀ x 1.5

4a

5

SAWFLIES contd.

1 *Rhogogaster viridis* catches other small insects on flowers, especially on umbellifer heads. The amount of black on the body varies, and the green fades quickly after death. Larva feeds on a wide range of plants. There are several similar species.

2 Turnip Sawfly (*Athalia rosae*) is distinguished from several similar species by the large amount of yellow on the thorax (underside completely yellow) together with the heavy black streak on the front edge of the forewings. Adults feed on pollen from a wide range of flowers, while larvae nibble the leaves of turnips, radishes and other brassicas, sometimes causing severe damage.

3 *Cephus pygmaeus* is one of several similar slender and rather lethargic species commonly seen feeding on the flower-heads of hawkweeds and other yellow composites. Larvae are virtually legless and tunnel in the stems of various grasses. Some species are important cereal pests.

4 *Allantus cinctus* is a predatory species, often capturing small flies and other insects on umbellifer heads It is one of several species mimicking various solitary wasps (*pages 152-6*). Larvae feed on strawberry and rose leaves.

5 Pine Sawfly (*Diprion pini*) is a serious forest pest. Its larvae – greyish green with black dots – destroy huge numbers of pine needles and young shoots each year, stunting or even killing the trees. Female is a little larger, usually with yellow bands on the abdomen, but only lightly toothed antennae.

4

.5

x 2.5

5 ♂

ASSORTED PARASITES

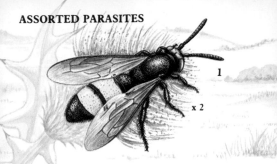

1

x 2

1 Scolia hirta is harmless to us despite its wasp-like appearance. Adults feed at flowers all over the southern half of Europe in summer and early autumn. Females search out grubs of chafer beetles (*pages 190-1*), paralyse them with a sting and lay an egg on each. The *Scolia* larvae then feed on their helpless hosts. Not found in Britain.

2 Chrysis ignita is one of the ruby-tails, whose larvae parasitise various solitary bees and wasps. It is most often seen scuttling over tree trunks in search of the host's nests.

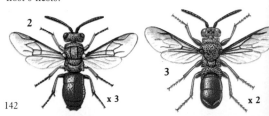

2

x 3

3

x 2

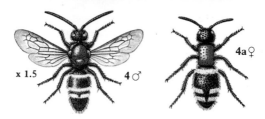

x 1.5   4♂   4a♀

3 *Parnopes grandior* is another ruby-tail, parasitising the grubs of *Bembix* wasps (*see page 154*). Notice the leaf-like flap at the rear of the thorax. Southern and central Europe, but not found in Britain.

4 Velvet Ant (*Mutilla europaea*) is not an ant at all, although the wingless female (**4a**) resembles one. Larvae live on the grubs of various bumblebees.

5 *Apanteles glomeratus*, a close relative of the ichneumons on the next page, is an important parasite of the large white butterfly or cabbage white. Eggs are laid in the caterpillar and the *Apanteles* grubs grow inside it. They leave the shrivelled caterpillar when they are fully grown and pupate in their own yellow cocoons around the dead body (**5a**).

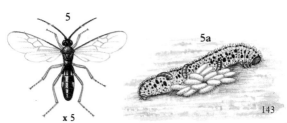

5

5a

x 5

ICHNEUMONS

The ichneumons are a very large group of rather slender parasites with long antennae. A lens will reveal at least 16 small segments to each antenna. The front edge of the forewing is distinctly thickened. Larvae generally develop in or on the young of other insects, but some develop in the egg cocoons of spiders. Adult female uses her antennae to smell out suitable hosts.

1 *Ophion luteus* is one of several similar species, some with dark patches at the rear end like *Netelia*, that commonly come to lights at night. Larvae develop in the caterpillars of butterflies and moths, which the female ichneumon pierces with her short ovipositor. The grub develops inside the host.

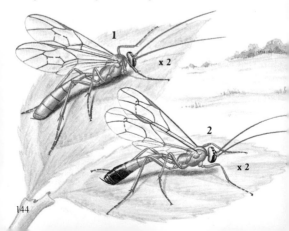

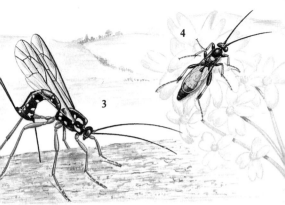

2 Netelia testacea resembles *Ophion* but is easily distinguished by the different wing venation. Related species often lack the black on the abdomen. The grubs develop on the outside of the host.

3 Rhyssa persuasoria has an enormously long ovipositor, with which she drills into pine trunks to lay her eggs on the grubs of the horntail (*page 137*). It is amazing how she detects the host in the wood, and how she drills with such slender equipment. The grub develops on the outside of its host.

4 Ichneumon suspiciosus can be found lapping nectar from umbellifers and other flowers from spring until late autumn. Adults hibernate and emerge to lay their eggs in the caterpillars of various moths in spring. There are several similar species.

GALL WASPS

Gall wasps are small ant-like insects, with or without wings, whose larvae live in plants and cause the development of the abnormal growths called galls. The tissue inside the galls provides nutritious food for the larvae. Wings, when present, have a distinctive venation. Many of the species have complex life stories, often involving two generations in a year with each generation causing a different kind of gall.

1 *Diplolepis rosae* causes the bedeguar gall or robin's pincushion on wild roses (**1a**). Inside each fluffy gall

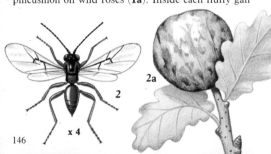

are several grubs, each in its own chamber. Adults emerge in spring and lay their eggs on the buds and young leaves. New galls grow as soon as the eggs hatch. Males are very rare and females can lay eggs without mating.

2 *Biorhiza pallida* causes the oak apple gall (**2a**). Winged adults emerge from the gall in mid-summer and, after mating, females enter the soil and lay their eggs on fine oak roots. Small round galls develop here and produce wingless females which climb the trees in spring and lay eggs without mating. The grubs hatching from these eggs cause more oak apples, from which the cycle begins again.

3 *Andricus kollari* causes the marble gall of oak (**3a**). Green at first, it becomes brown and woody in autumn and the gall wasp emerges through a neat hole. All the insects at this stage are females, laying eggs on the buds without mating. The full life cycle involves the Turkey oak, where male and female insects develop in tiny galls in the buds.

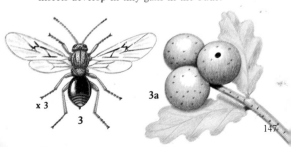

x 3

3

3a

147

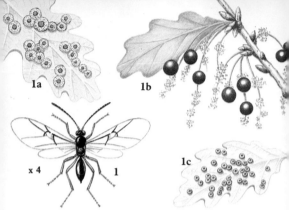

GALL WASPS contd.

1 *Neuroterus quercusbaccarum* induces the formation of two very different galls on oak. Common spangle galls (**1a**) appear under the leaves in late summer, falling with the leaves and producing non-mating females in spring. These lay eggs in the buds and the resulting larvae cause the formation of currant galls (**1b**) on the catkins and young leaves. Male and female insects emerge from these galls in mid-summer and mated females lay eggs that give rise to the spangle galls again. Silk button spangle galls (**1c**) are caused by the autumn generation of a very similar species *Neuroterus numismalis*. The summer galls of this species are insignificant little swellings in the leaves.

ANTS

Ants are social insects, living in colonies ruled by one or more queens. The workforce consists of sterile, wingless females, generally much smaller than the queens. Winged ants appear only in the mating season, when males and potential new queens swarm. Only a few mated females ever get to be queens, always breaking off their wings before settling down.

2 Wood Ant (*Formica rufa*) builds large mounds of leaves and twigs in light woodland (**2c**). Each colony contains several queens (**2a**) and perhaps 250,000 workers (**2b**) which forage relentlessly from spring to autumn – mainly for insects and honeydew. They have no sting, but fire formic acid at intruders. Mating swarms appear in early summer.

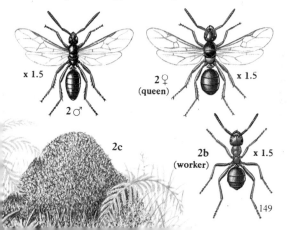

x 1.5

2 ♂

2 ♀
(queen)

x 1.5

2c

2b
(worker)

x 1.5

ANTS contd.

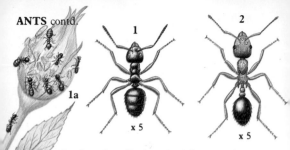

x 5

x 5

1 Black Garden Ant (*Lasius niger*) is one of our commonest species, often nesting under garden paths and even town pavements. Notice the one-segmented waist bearing a little upright scale. There is no sting. Like most ants, it is very fond of honeydew (*see page 90*) and is often seen 'milking' aphids for this sugary liquid (**1a**). It also eats a wide range of small insects. Mating flights occur in July and August, with winged males and females pouring from the ground in hundreds and taking to the air like columns of smoke.

2 *Myrmica rubra*, also very common in the garden, is one of the red ants. It has a sting and a two-

x 2

segmented waist. Its behaviour is much like that of the last species, but it prefers to nest under small stones or logs. The colonies are smaller than those of the last species and also differ in having several queens.

3 *Messor barbara* is one of the harvesting ants which feed mainly on seeds. The workers drag the seeds back to the nest from considerable distances and a task force with extra-large heads cracks them open. The empty husks are discarded all around the nest. Some seeds get dropped or thrown out as well, and the nest entrance may be surrounded by seedlings. This is a southern species, not found in Britain.

4 *Camponotus vagus* is one of Europe's largest ants, nesting in fallen trees and other timber. Workers can often be seen rushing in and out of cracks in old fences. It is an omnivorous species, but with a particular liking for honeydew. It has no sting. It lives only in southern Europe, although several similar species occur further north as well. None lives in Britain.

4

x 2

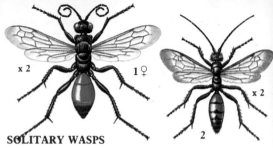

SOLITARY WASPS

Solitary wasps do not live in colonies like the more familiar wasps (*page 159*) that buzz around us in late summer. Each female makes and provisions a nest just for her own offspring. The nests are commonly in the ground or in dead wood and many of the species are known as digger wasps. Insects or spiders are used to provision the nests after being paralysed by the sting.

1 *Cryptocheilus affinis* is one of the spider-hunting wasps, a group distinguished from the digger wasps by the way in which the pronotum (*see Introduction*) extends back to the wing bases. Female antennae often coil up after death. Male is often much smaller. Female spider-hunters dig several nest burrows and provision each with a single spider and a single egg.

2 *Anoplius viaticus* is another spider-hunter. It chases and catches wolf spiders (*pages 222-3*). Like many others in its group, it is often seen in the spring lapping nectar from flowers, especially umbellifers.

3 Bee-killer (*Philanthus triangulum*) is a true digger wasp, with the pronotum not reaching back to the wing bases. Black triangles on abdomen may be very small or even absent. It catches honey bees and carries them back to its burrow slung under its body (**3a**). Rare in Britain and absent from northern Europe.

4 *Ammophila pubescens* is one of a group of slender diggers known as sand wasps. It nests in sandy ground and stocks its burrows with non-hairy caterpillars. If these are not too big it will fly home with them: otherwise it drags them over the ground. Unlike most digger wasps, it adds more prey to the burrows from time to time.

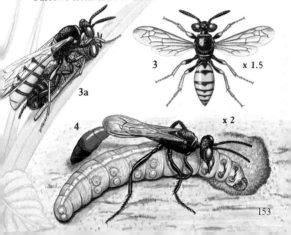

3a

3   x 1.5

4   x 2

1 ♀ x 2

DIGGER WASPS contd.

1 *Crabro cribrarius* is one of several similar digger wasps and is not uncommon in gardens, especially on sandy soils. It nests in the ground, or occasionally in rotting logs and tree stumps, and stocks its nest with assorted flies. Like most digger wasps, it puts several victims into its nest and, because they are only paralysed, they do not rot and last until the wasp larvae have finished growing. Males in this genus have enlarged, plate-like front legs.

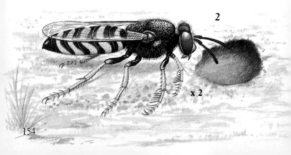

2

x 2

2 Bembix rostrata also specialises in flies. Females dig a burrow in sandy soil with the aid of a particularly well developed 'rake' on their front legs.(Many female diggers have a rake, but it is not always as well developed as in *Bembix*, and some males also have a small rake or comb.) Instead of stocking the nest completely at the start, they return to top it up from time to time, usually bringing larger flies as the grubs get bigger. *Bembix* resembles the social wasps at first sight, but is easily distinguished by the way in which the wings are held flat over the body at rest. Not found in Britain.

3 Sphex maxillosus is one of several similar species that stock their nests with crickets and grasshoppers. The victims are immobilised with two or three well-placed stings and then dragged back to the nest burrow as shown below. The wasp uses one of the victim's antennae as a tow-rope and can haul its prize up remarkably steep slopes. Not found in Britain.

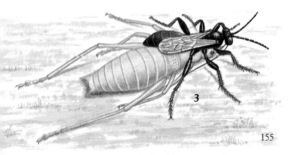

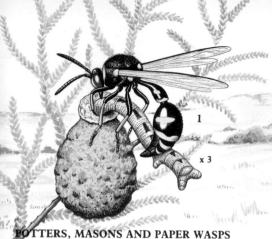

1

x 3

POTTERS, MASONS AND PAPER WASPS

1 Potter Wasp (*Eumenes coarctatus*) is a solitary species, but more closely related to the social wasps than to the diggers. As in the social wasps, the pronotum reaches back to the wing bases and the wings are folded longitudinally at rest, thus exposing much of the abdomen. The potter wasp, identified by its characteristically shaped narrow waist, lives mainly on heathland, where females build little vase-shaped nests from mud. They lay an egg in each and stock them with small caterpillars before sealing the nest and going off to build another – sometimes attached to the first.

2 *Ancistrocerus parietinus* is one of several very similar solitary species known as mason wasps. Using sand and mud, often moistened with saliva, females build a number of small cells in some kind of cavity or secluded crevice. Old walls are favourite sites but hollow stems are also used. Each cell receives an egg and is then stocked with small caterpillars.

3 Paper Wasp (*Polistes gallicus*) is one of the social wasps, but it builds only small colonies. Its flat or slightly domed nest is built with paper made from chewed wood pulp, just like that of the other social wasps, but has no outer covering. It is fixed to plants or rocks and is commonly found in or on buildings. Away from the nest, the wasp – one of several similar species – can be recognised by the tapering front of the abdomen. Does not live in Britain.

x 1.5

2

3

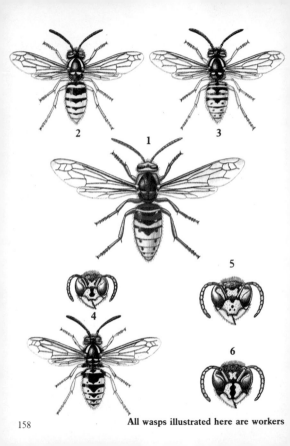

158

All wasps illustrated here are workers

SOCIAL WASPS

Our social wasps, which include the familiar garden species, live in annual colonies, each founded and ruled by a queen. Several thousand workers, smaller than the queens, may be reared in the paper nests. Males, recognised by their longer antennae, appear in summer. Larvae are fed with chewed insects and other animal matter, the cells not being mass-provisioned as in most solitary species. Prey is rarely stung, for the sting is primarily defensive. Only newly mated queens survive the winter, often hibernating in houses. Most species nest in the ground or in various cavities.

1 Hornet (*Vespa crabro*), Europe's largest wasp, nests mainly in hollow trees, but also uses wall cavities.

2 Tree Wasp (*Dolichovespula sylvestris*) has two yellow spots on the thorax and a reddish abdominal tinge. The face has a dark vertical bar, occasionally anchor-shaped.

3 Red Wasp (*Vespula rufa*) has two yellow spots on the thorax and a reddish abdominal tinge. The face has a dark vertical bar, occasionally anchor-shaped.

4 Common Wasp (*Vespula vulgaris*) has four yellow spots at the rear of the thorax and an anchor-like mark on the face. The thoracic stripes are parallel-sided.

5 German Wasp (*Vespula germanica*) is like the last species but the face pattern differs and the thoracic stripes bulge in the middle.

6 Norwegian Wasp (*Dolichovespula norvegica*) is like the tree wasp apart from the dark face bar.

SOLITARY BEES

Bees are mostly rather hairy insects, all feeding on pollen and nectar and playing a very important role in pollinating flowers. Most are solitary species, with life histories like those of the solitary wasps (*page 152*) except that their nests are stocked with pollen and nectar. With the exception of a few primitive species, the females have special pollen-collecting equipment on their legs or bodies. Nectar is carried home in the stomach. Many species later modify the nectar and turn it into honey. Some nest in pre-existing cavities, especially hollow stems, while others dig their own – in the ground or dead wood as a rule. A few species build clay pots in which to lay their eggs.

1 *Colletes halophilus* digs nest burrows in sandy soil, mainly near the coast. Each burrow has several cells, plastered with an oral secretion that cements the sand

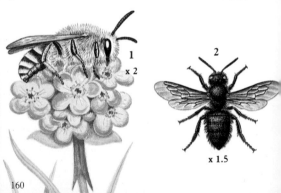

1
x 2

2

x 1.5

grains together. Large numbers of these bees may cluster on seaside plants in summer.

2 *Chalicodoma parietina* builds small clay capsules and attaches them to walls and stones. Each capsule contains one egg and a supply of food. Male has clear wings and browner hair. Not found in Britain or northern Europe.

3 *Osmia rufa* is very common in spring and early summer. Female (**3a**) is larger than the male and can be recognised by two small black horns on her head. She commonly chooses walls for nesting (**3b**), but will use any suitable cavity and has been known to nest in key holes and snail shells. She uses mud to build small cells in the chosen cavity.

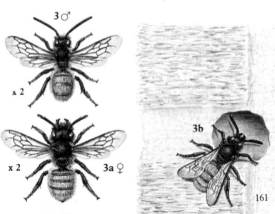

3♂

x 2

x 2   3a ♀

3b

1

x 2

SOLITARY BEES contd.

1 *Anthidium manicatum*, easily recognised by its abdominal pattern, nests in pre-existing holes in wood, rocks or brickwork. The nest is lined with hairs gathered from plants. The hairs are rolled into a ball and carried home under the body. There are several similar species on the continent but this is the only one in Britain. Unlike most bees, males are significantly larger than females. Some species line their nests with resin collected from conifers instead of with plant hairs.

2 Leaf-cutter Bee (*Megachile centuncularis*) constructs its nest cells with leaf segments, neatly cut from living plants by the female. Each segment is usually semi-circular and is carried home rolled up under the

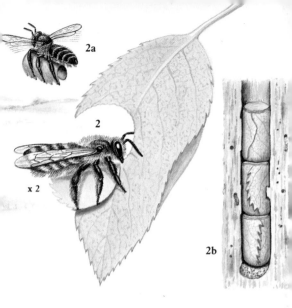

female's body (**2a**). The segments are then neatly glued together to make a series of sausage-shaped cells in a hollow stem or other suitable cavity (**2b**). Notice the bright orange hairs under the female's abdomen. These form her pollen brush, on which she carries back the pollen. Wild and cultivated roses are the main targets of this species, which is the commonest of several closely related ones.

SOLITARY BEES contd.

1 *Andrena fulva* is one of a large group of ground-nesters known as mining bees. Females, very easily recognised by their bright coat, can be seen feeding at currant and gooseberry flowers and other blossom early in spring. Males are smaller and darker and much less hairy. The nest, often in the lawn, is surrounded by a cone of excavated soil.

2 *Andrena haemorrhoa* is another mining bee, displaying the rather flat abdomen common in this group. It is one of the earliest to appear in spring, visiting sallow and dandelion flowers among many others. Most mining bees appear quite early in the year and play a major role in pollinating fruit trees. Some have a second brood in summer.

3 *Eucera longicornis* has extremely long antennae in the male. All male bees have longer antennae than the females – with 13 segments instead of 12 – but in

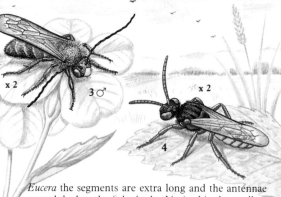

x 2

3 ♂

x 2

4

Eucera the segments are extra long and the antennae exceed the length of the body. Notice his clear yellow face. Female has normal antennae, broader pale bands on her abdomen and much hairier legs. She nests in the ground.

4 *Nomada fulvicornis* is almost hairless and more like a wasp than a bee in appearance. Female has no pollen-gathering apparatus and lays her eggs in the nests of various mining bees. Her larvae kill the rightful occupants and eat the stored food themselves. *Nomada* is thus known as a cuckoo bee. There are several similar species, easily distinguished from the social wasps by their smaller size and by holding their wings flat over the body at rest. Distinction from the digger wasps (*page 154*) is less easy in the field, but the bees' antennae are largely red or brown instead of black.

1 Xylocopa violacea is the commonest of four similar species in southern and central Europe. Its colouring makes it very conspicuous as it flies rapidly and noisily from flower to flower. Like most bees, it will sting if handled roughly but it is not an insect to be feared. Most numerous in summer and autumn, it hibernates as an adult and re-appears in spring when the female excavates a nest burrow in dead wood. Apart from occasional vagrants, it does not occur in Britain.

2 Anthophora plumipes displays such a marked difference between the sexes that they are often thought to be two different species. Female (**2a**) can be recognised by her jet black coat and the rust-coloured pollen brushes on her back legs, although these brushes are obscured by their heavy loads of pollen when the bee is foraging. Male is best recognised by the tufts of long hairs on his middle legs, but his white face is a good clue when he is in flight. Although this bee is often mistaken for a bumblebee, its flight is very different – much faster, with many darting movements and much hovering and a much higher flight tone. It appears early in spring and uses its very long tongue to collect nectar from deep-throated flowers. It is very common in gardens. Females excavate a nest burrow in the ground or in soft mortar. Where several females decide to excavate close together – the result of a suitable site, not a desire for company – they can do much damage to old walls.

2 ♂
x 1.5
x 1.5
2a ♀

HONEY BEES

1 Honey Bee (*Apis mellifera*) differs from superficially similar bees in its very long and slender apical cell which reaches almost to the wing-tip. Notice also the very broad hind legs: the worker's tibia is fringed with stout hairs to form the pollen basket (**1c**). When free of pollen the outer surface of the tibia is very shiny. A native of southern Asia, the bee has been taken to many parts of the world for the sake of its honey. Many races exist, differing in abdominal pattern. Those shown here are of the Italian race. The Honey bee is a strongly social insect, with a long-lived queen (**1a**) ruling each colony. Several thousand workers (**1b**) build the nest, collect food, and do all the other chores, including making honey from nectar. Water is removed from the nectar and various chemical changes also occur during the process. Males or drones appear in summer and mate with any new queens that appear. Queens can do nothing but lay eggs and, except when on their mating flights, are always surrounded by attentive workers. New queens are reared when the reigning monarch begins to age and also when the population outgrows the nest. In the latter instance the old queen flies off with a swarm of workers to begin a new colony elsewhere, leaving a new queen to take charge of the old colony. Natural nesting sites are usually in hollow trees, but some nests are built in the open (**1d**). They consist of vertical wax combs, each with thousands of hexagonal cells used for rearing grubs or storing food. The insects readily build in hives, for as far as the bees are concerned these are just like hollow trees.

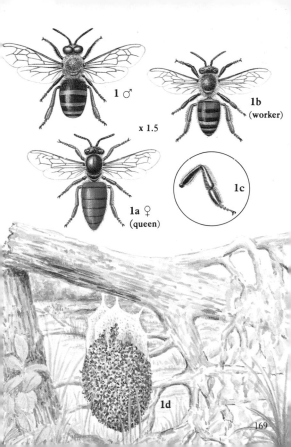

1 ♂

x 1.5

1b
(worker)

1a ♀
(queen)

1c

1d

BUMBLEBEES

Bumblebees live in annual colonies rather like the social wasps, with only the newly-mated queens surviving the winter to start new colonies in spring. Most build nests of grass or moss on or under the ground, often making use of old mouse holes. Inside the nest they make relatively simple wax cells in which to rear their grubs on a mixture of pollen and honey. The first spring workers are very small. Pollen is carried in pollen baskets on the back legs, just as in the honey bee (*page 168*), and a fully-laden bee may struggle to get airborne.

1 *Bombus lucorum*, an early spring bee of gardens and hedgerows, has clear lemon yellow bands on the thorax and the front of the abdomen.

2 *Bombus lapidarius* queens and workers can be distinguished from most other bumblebees by the red 'tail' and the black pollen basket. Male has a yellow collar.

3 *Bombus pascuorum* has a rather thin coat ranging from almost black to a bright foxy red. It is still active in late autumn, when other species have gone.

4 *Bombus alpinus* identified by its coat colour and very black hind legs, flies in alpine pastures and also on the heathlands of Scandinavia.

5 *Psithyrus barbutellus* is a cuckoo bee wth no worker caste. Female lays her eggs in nests of the bumblebee *Bombus hortorum* and relies on the workers of that species to rear her grubs. Notice that there are no pollen baskets. The coat is also thinner than in bumblebees and the wings are darker.

These are all queens. The workers are generally somewhat smaller

5

4

x 1.5

x 1.5

BEETLES

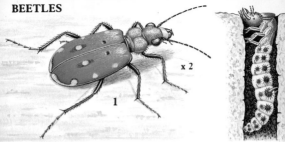

With about 250,000 known species, the beetles are the largest of all the insect orders. All have biting mouths and the forewings, known as elytra, are generally tough and horny, usually meeting in a neat line down the middle of the back. They allow the beetles to burrow or scramble about on the ground without harming the delicate hind wings. In flight, the forewings are held rigidly to the sides and not moved up and down. Many beetles, however, are flightless, with no hind wings. Some lack forewings as well. The group contains carnivores, vegetarians – including many important pests – and scavengers. Larvae, which are extremely varied in form, often use the same food as the adults.

1 Green Tiger Beetle (*Cicindela campestris*) flies noisily in the sunshine, especially in open, sandy habitats. It does not fly far, however, and spends most of its time basking on the ground. It feeds on a wide range of other insects, which it grabs with its large jaws. Larva (**1a**) lives in a vertical shaft with its jaws at the surface ready to snatch any insect that walks by.

2 Wood Tiger Beetle (*Cicindela sylvatica*) behaves like the previous species and is found in dry wooded areas as well as on heathland. There are several other tiger beetles, all with a similar shape and all very fast runners.

3 Bombardier Beetle (*Brachinus crepitans*) is one of the very large group known as ground beetles – long-legged, fast-running predators. It lives in dry, sunny places and gets its name for its ability to fire a volatile, caustic liquid from its hind end when alarmed. The firing is accompanied by a small bang and is quite enough to deter small enemies.

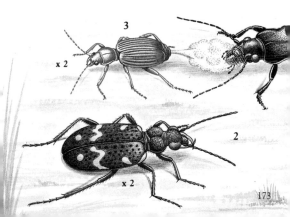

GROUND BEETLES

1 Violet Ground Beetle (*Carabus violaceus*) can often be found under logs and stones during the daytime, the violet sheen around the margins of the thorax and elytra distinguishing it from a number of close relatives. It emerges at night to hunt for slugs and other small creatures and also enjoys ripe fruit. Notice the long legs and oval shape characteristic of many members of this group. Like many other ground beetles, it has no hind wings and is quite unable to fly. Larva (**1a**) captures prey on or under the ground.

2 *Carabus nemoralis* resembles the last species but the elytra have a brassy or bronzy sheen and bear rows of small but distinct pits. Both species can be found in the garden.

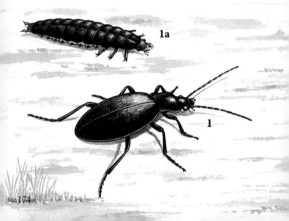

1a

1

3 *Amara aenea* has a smoother outline than many ground beetles, with a brassy or bluish green sheen to the elytra. Living in dry, open habitats with short vegetation, it feeds largely on vegetable matter. It is fully winged and able to fly.

4 *Pterostichus madidus* is a flightless, nocturnal species, abundant in gardens and other cultivated areas, where it takes a good deal of vegetable food and is especially fond of strawberries. It can be distinguished from many similar species by its largely chestnut legs and the blunt hind angles of the pronotum. Larva is similar to that of the Violet Ground Beetle, but a good deal narrower.

x 5

x 4

1

2

GROUND BEETLES contd. and WATER BEETLES

1 *Notiophilus biguttatus* is one of several closely related species with protruding eyes and a flattened body. It is a flightless, but fast-running and sun-loving insect of open habitats, including gardens. The deep brassy sheen on the elytra may mask the pattern from some angles.

2 *Callistus lunatus* is a sun-loving species of dry grassland. Although fully winged, it spends most of its time scurrying about on the ground, often at remarkable speed. The dark areas have either green or blue iridescence. It is rare in Britain and absent from northern Europe.

Water beetles, with few exceptions, remain air-breathing and have to surface periodically to renew the supplies carried under the elytra. They belong to two main groups: one comes up tail-first for air and the other head-first. Most can fly well if necessary.

3 Great Diving Beetle (*Dytiscus marginalis*) is a carnivorous species of still and slow-moving water. It rises tail-first for air. Males have swollen front legs and smooth elytra, while the elytra of females (**3a**) are ribbed. The green colour disappears after death. It can be distinguished from several related species by the yellow margin all around the pronotum. Larva (**3b**), known as the water tiger for its fierce habits, pierces prey with its hollow jaws and sucks them dry. Like the adult, it will attack even frogs and fishes.

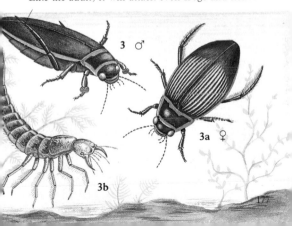

WATER BEETLES contd.

1 Whirligig Beetle (*Gyrinus natator*) is named for its habit of zooming round in circles on the water surface. Each eye is in two halves: one looks down into the water, the other across the surface. It feeds mainly on mosquito larvae and dives when alarmed. There are several similar species.

2 Great Silver Beetle (*Hydrous piceus*) is one of Europe's largest beetles. It rises head-first for air and carries a reservoir enclosed by hairs on its underside as well as the normal air tank under the elytra. This gives its underside a very silvery appearance in the water. A sharp spine under the thorax can spike your finger! A poor swimmer, it lives in weedy ponds, feeding mainly on plant debris but also attacking water snails. Larvae feed almost entirely on water snails.

3 *Platambus maculatus* is easily recognised by its pattern. A predatory species, it lives mainly in running water. It rises tail-first for air.

4 *Haliplus fulvus* has very convex elytra decorated with rows of elongate depressions. A poor swimmer, it crawls about in weedy ponds and feeds on algae. It rises tail-first for air.

5 Screech Beetle (*Hygrobia herrmanni*), recognised by its convex body and large eyes, squeaks loudly when alarmed – when caught in a net, for example. It feeds on invertebrates in muddy ponds and rises tail-first for air. Absent from northern Europe.

BURYING BEETLES

1 *Nicrophorus vespilloides* is one of several very similar species known as sexton or burying beetles. They feed on the carcases of birds and small mammals, which they find with the aid of scent detectors on their clubbed antennae. In the breeding season male and female work together to bury a carcase by digging the soil from under it. Female then lays eggs close to the carcase and the grubs feed on the decaying flesh and also on fly larvae and other scavengers that develop there. Related species, with slight differences in elytral patterns, generally have orange tips to their antennae.

2 *Nicrophorus humator* is easily recognised by its all-black elytra – strongly truncated as in all members of the genus – and orange antennal clubs. Like the

other sexton beetles, it flies mainly by night and is a common visitor to the moth-collector's light trap.

3 *Oiceoptoma thoracicum* has three distinct ridges on each silky elytron. It feeds on insect grubs in dung and carrion, but does not bury the material. It lives mainly in woodland.

4 *Silpha atrata* preys on snails, pushing its narrow head deep into their shells to consume the soft flesh. Notice the rather glossy and strongly ribbed elytra. It occurs mainly in damp, shady places – where it has no problem in finding food.

x 1.5

ROVE BEETLES

The rove beetles are a very large group in which the elytra are very short, leaving most of the abdomen exposed. Despite the short elytra, however, the hind wings are generally fully developed and most species fly well. The majority are carnivores and scavengers and many can be found in dung and carrion.

1 Devil's Coach-horse (*Staphylinus olens*), one of the largest rove beetles, is also known as the cock-tail for the way in which it raises its abdomen when alarmed. This threatening appearance is re-inforced by the huge gaping jaws. Common in gardens and out-buildings as well as in many natural habitats, it emerges from cover at night to hunt a variety of invertebrates. It destroys a good number of slugs in the garden.

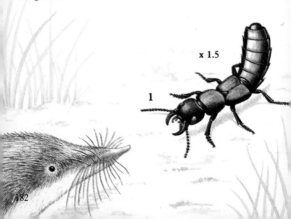

x 1.5

1

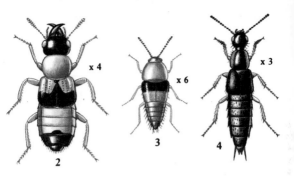

2 *Oxyporus rufus* can be recognised by its large, forward-pointing jaws – about as long as the rest of the head – and its strongly arched body. Both adults and larvae live in woodland fungi.

3 *Tachyporus obtusus* is one of many rather similar species with strongly tapered abdomen and a distinctly smooth, shuttle-shaped outline, but can be distinguished from most by its uniformly orange pronotum. Notice the bi-coloured elytra typical of this genus. It is found mainly amongst mosses and leaf litter in woodlands and other shady places.

4 *Philonthus marginatus* lives with many other members of this genus in dung and decaying vegetation – including the garden compost heap. It is readily distinguished from its relatives by the orange sides to its thorax.

ROVE BEETLES contd.

1 *Emus hirtus* is a large and unmistakable rove beetle with a dense fur coat. It occurs mainly on sunny pastures and other grassland and you are most likely to find it near cow-pats and other dung or around the carcases of small mammals. It feeds on the other insects that come to scavenge on the decaying matter. Unlike most other large rove beetles, it is often active by day.

2 *Creophilus maxillosus* is another easily recognised species, with an abdominal pattern of grey and black hairs. It has similar habits to those of *Emus*, although it can be found in a wider variety of habitats and has a distinct preference for hunting on carrion. It also frequents rotting vegetation and is considerably more common than the last species.

3 *Stenus bimaculatus* is one of several similar species with large, bulging eyes. It is a sun-loving beetle, living in damp places, and it can skim over water surfaces by exuding an oily secretion from the rear. It feeds on a variety of small insects, especially springtails.

4 *Paederus littoralis* is a flightless predator of other small insects. It lives mainly on river banks and in other damp places, although it also occurs in dry grassland. The elytra are generally deep metallic blue, sometimes appearing virtually black.

5 *Hister impressus* is not closely related to the rove beetles, although the elytra are somewhat truncated. It is abundant on carrion and in dung and other rotting matter, where it feeds mainly on fly grubs and other scavenging insects. Larvae feed in the same way. There are several similar species, some with red spots on the elytra. They have varied tooth patterns on the front legs.

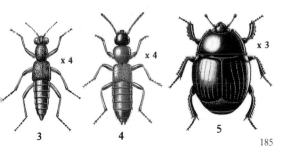

3   4   5

STAG BEETLES

1 Stag Beetle (*Lucanus cervus*), one of Europe's largest beetles, is named for the antler-like jaws of the males, who use them for grappling with each other just like deer. Females (**1a**) have no antlers. Both sexes fly well, usually in the early evening, and enjoy feeding on sap oozing from damaged trees. Their size varies a great deal, depending on the quality of the larval food. Larvae are large white, C-shaped grubs, not unlike those of the cockchafer (*page 190*). They live in decaying tree stumps and other timber, mainly oak.

2 Lesser Stag Beetle (*Dorcus parallelipipedus*) has no antlers and resembles a female stag beetle, but it is flatter and blacker. The middle tibiae provide sure proof of identity, with just one small tooth on each instead of three as in the previous species. Larvae develop in rotting deciduous timber.

3 *Sinodendron cylindricum* also breeds in decaying deciduous timber. Males are easily recognised by the horn on the head, but females have just a small bump. The body size is extremely variable, according to larval diet. Larvae often live communally and adults sometimes emerge in swarms on summer evenings. Like the previous two species, this beetle takes two or more years to complete its development.

4 *Aphodius rufipes* is one of the dung beetles (*see page 188*). It is abundant in and on cow pats, but it does not bury the dung like many of its relatives. Active by night, it is a common visitor to lighted windows and also the the moth-collector's light trap.

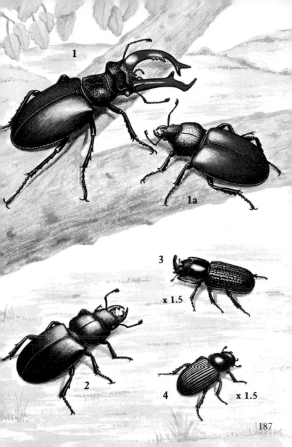

1

1a

3

x 1.5

2

4 x 1.5

DUNG BEETLES

Dung beetles are related to the chafers (*page 190*). All have antennae with a club composed of several flaps which can be opened like a fan to increase the receptive area. Both adult and larval dung beetles feed on mammalian dung, the adults using their rake-like front legs for digging into the dung and often for burying it as well.

1 Dor Beetle (*Geotrupes stercorarius*) is one of several similar species with a bluish or greenish sheen. The jaws are clearly visible from above. It lives in cow dung and the female digs shafts below it to depths of about 60cm. The male takes dung down the shafts, where female packs it into side chambers and lays her eggs on it.

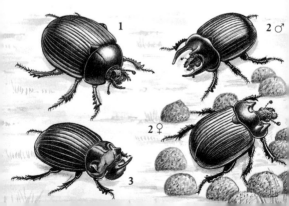

2 Minotaur Beetle (*Typhaeus typhoeus*) breeds on sheep and rabbit dung, burying the pellets as much as 150cm below the surface in sandy areas. Male is easily recognised by his three horns. Female has only two small points. The jaws are clearly visible from above. It is most active in the evening and, like the other dung beetles shown here, it flies strongly.

3 *Copris lunaris* has a smaller horn in females. It tunnels under cow pats and the female stands guard over her eggs and larvae in the dung-filled burrows.

4 *Scarabaeus semipunctatus* is one of the scarabs. The pitted pronotum and smooth elytra separate it from several related species, all from southern Europe. The jaws are concealed from above. Standing on its front legs, it trundles balls of dung along with its hind legs. Male and female work together to bury dung in suitable places for their larvae, but individuals also bury balls for personal consumption.

189

CHAFER BEETLES

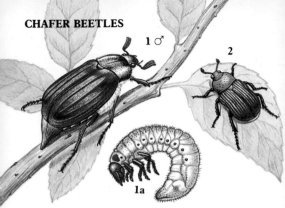

Chafers are vegetarian relatives of the dung beetles. Notice the fan-like antennal clubs – larger in males than in females – and the truncated elytra of most species. Many are serious pests.

1 Cockchafer (*Melolontha melolontha*) is also called the May-bug. It flies in May and June, often crashing into lights at night. Adults chew the leaves of trees and shrubs, while larvae (**1a**) live in the soil and cause much damage to crop roots.

2 Garden Chafer (*Phyllopertha horticola*) behaves like the cockchafer but prefers to fly in the sun. The elytra may have a green or blue sheen.

3 Rose Chafer (*Cetonia aurata*) is rather flat and its elytra may be bronze. The underside is coppery red.

Adults nibble all kinds of flowers, usually in the sunshine, while larvae feed in decaying wood.

4 Bee Beetle (*Trichius fasciatus*) is usually seen in flowers. Its pattern varies a good deal, with the yellow areas sometimes deep orange. Larva feeds in rotting wood. Rare in Britain.

5 Pine Chafer (*Polyphylla fullo*) is found in areas with light, sandy soils. Adults chew pine needles, while larvae feed on the roots of grasses and similar plants. Adult can screech loudly by rubbing the tips of the elytra against the abdomen. It does not occur in Britain or northern Europe.

SOLDIER BEETLES and GLOW-WORMS

1 *Cantharis rustica* is a very common member of a group whose bright 'uniforms' have given them the name of soldier and sailor beetles. The elytra are rather soft. There are several similar species, differing slightly in the colour of the thorax and the legs. They are predatory beetles, active by day and catching a variety of small insects on flowers – especially on the domed heads of the umbellifers. They fly well in warm weather. Larvae are also predatory, hunting mainly on the ground and resembling those of the ground beetles (*page 174*).

2 *Rhagonycha fulva* is closely related to the previous species and has similar habits. It is often known as the bloodsucker because of its colour – but it is quite harmless to us.

3 Firefly (*Luciola lusitanica*) is a soft-winged beetle with light-producing organs under the tip of the

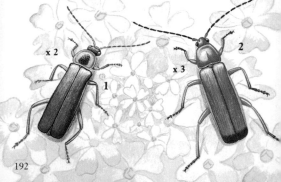

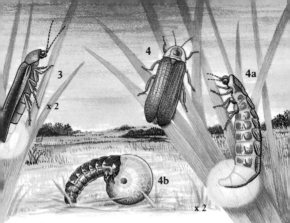

abdomen. Both sexes are fully winged, but the female does not fly. She sits in the grass and replies by flashing her light when males flash their signals overhead. The male, who has larger eyes and a less pointed tail, then drops down to mate. Flashes are produced about once a second, and a field full of fireflies is a marvellous sight after dark. Larva feeds on snails. The firefly lives in southern Europe east of the Rhône.

4 Glow-worm (*Lampyris noctiluca*) is related to the firefly but only the female glows. She is wingless (**4a**) and she keeps her greenish light on for long periods. Males fly overhead and drop down to mate when they see the light. Larvae resemble the female and feed on snails (**4b**).

CLICK BEETLES and OTHERS

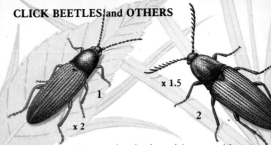

The click beetles are shuttle-shaped insects with an unusual way of righting themselves when turned on their backs. They arch their backs strongly, and powerful muscles then throw them into the air with a loud click. With luck, they land the right way up.

1 *Athous haemorrhoidalis* is one of the commonest click beetles, displaying the drab colours common to most of the group. It is especially common on grassland, where its larva (**1a**) feeds on roots. Known as wireworms, many clickworm larvae are serious pests of farm and garden.

2 *Ctenicera cuprea*, sometimes entirely violet or copper-coloured, has much smaller teeth on the antennae of the female. This click beetle occurs in rough grassland, mainly in northern areas, where larvae feed on roots.

3 *Ampedus sanguineus* is one of the more brightly coloured click beetles. A rare species, it breeds in dead and decaying timber, especially conifers.

4 *Trichodes alvearius* is a rather hairy beetle with blue or black bands on the elytra. The front band is U-shaped, but almost straight in the otherwise similar *Trichodes apiarius*. Adults feed at flowers, while larvae feed on the grubs of various solitary bees. Not found in Britain or northern Europe.

5 *Thanasimus formicarius* can be found on tree trunks in spring. Adults and larvae feed on bark beetle grubs on various kinds of trees. They are abundant in elms affected by Dutch elm disease.

x 2

1

x 2

2

BEETLES contd.

1 *Capnodis tenebrionis* is a striking, but rare beetle, sometimes found sunbathing on blackthorn and plum foliage. Larvae tunnel in the older stems of these trees. Does not live in Britain or northern Europe.

2 *Anthaxia hungarica* frequents summer flowers in and around oakwoods. Male is almost entirely green. Female elytra are green or bluish. Larva lives in decaying oaks. This is a sun-loving species from southern and central Europe. Not found in Britain.

3 *Lampra rutilans* has a golden or bluish sheen, generally with a reddish tinge on the outer edges of the elytra. The black markings are of variable extent and may be absent. Larvae are tadpole-shaped, as in all the species shown here, and live under the bark of

old lime trees. Adults can be seen flying around the trees in the sunshine in early summer. The beetle does not live in Britain.

4 *Agrilus pannonicus* is dark green or blue, often with a brassy tinge. There is always a patch of white hair near the tip of each elytron and there may be other small white patches. It flies in the sunshine. Larvae feed under the bark of old oaks, and adults are generally found on and around the same trees.

5 *Chrysobothris affinis* is most often seen basking on logs and felled trees in deciduous woodland in summer. The front spot may be missing from each elytron. Larvae feed under the bark of various trees – mainly old and ailing ones – and occasionally cause damage in orchards. Not found in Britain.

FABRIC and TIMBER BEETLES

1 *Tenebrio molitor* is flightless, with its elytra fused together. Sometimes found out of doors in summer, it occurs mainly in buildings, where it feeds on cereal products and is sometimes a serious pest. It is nocturnal and superficially like a ground beetle, but distinguished by its slightly clubbed antennae. Larva (**1a**) is the mealworm, widely used as food for cagebirds and other pets.

2 Furniture Beetle (*Anobium punctatum*) is the adult of the infamous woodworm, which does so much damage tunnelling through our furniture and other household timbers. Adults emerge through neat exit holes about 2mm across (**2a**) and can often be seen on window panes in summer. Notice how the head is completely hidden under a hood. The shape of the antennae helps to identify this pest.

3 Death-Watch Beetle (*Xestobium rufovillosum*) is a larger relative of the last species, usually breeding in old oak timbers – especially those that are slightly damp – and found mainly in old buildings. Its exit holes (**3a**) are 3-4mm across. Like the last species, it also breeds in dead and dying timber in the wild.

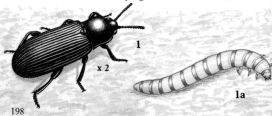

1

x 2

1a

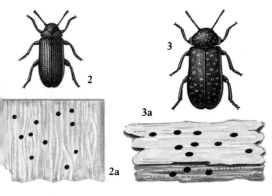

4 Anthrenus verbasci is one of the carpet beetles. Several similar species feed at flowers in summer. Larvae (**4a**), known as woolly bears, cause severe damage to carpets and other household fabrics and also chew through insect collections.

5 Attagenus pellio behaves like the last species, but larva has a very long tuft of hair at the rear. Both species commonly breed in birds' nests.

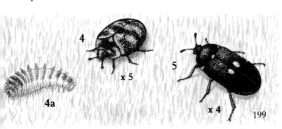

199

LADYBIRD BEETLES

1 *Endomychus coccineus* merely resembles the ladybirds. Flatter and lacking clubbed antennae, it eats fungi under bark of dead or dying trees.

Ladybirds are mostly predators. Both adults and larvae feed largely on aphids. Their bright coats warn of their bitter taste. Handle one and you will detect a pungent fluid. Adults often hibernate in large masses.

2 7-spot Ladybird (*Coccinella 7-punctata*) is one of our largest and commonest species. Larvae (**2a**) and pupae (**2b**) abound on aphid-infested plants.

3 2-spot Ladybird (*Adalia bipunctata*) is sometimes black with red spots, especially in northern areas. The legs are always black.

4 22-spot Ladybird (*Thea 22-punctata*) abounds on vegetation, feeding mainly on mildews on the leaves.

5 14-spot Ladybird (*Propylea 14-punctata*), ranges from almost all yellow with widely separated black spots to virtually all black.

6 Eyed Ladybird (*Anatis ocellata*) named for its eye-like spots, lives on and around conifers.

1

x 5

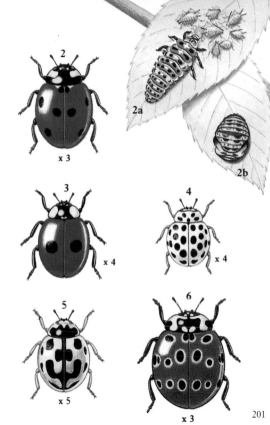

201

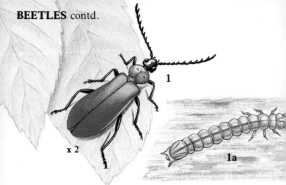

1

x 2

1a

1 Pyrochroa coccinea is one of the cardinal beetles, which all display brilliant red coats. They are most often seen sunning themselves on leaves and flowers in wooded areas. Larva (**1a**) is extremely flat and feeds on a variety of other insects under the bark of dead and dying trees. *Pyrochroa serraticornis* is almost identical but has a red head.

2 Oedemera nobilis is a pollen-feeding beetle abundant on flowers in spring and summer. The elytra are soft, often bluish, and always gaping – more so in male than in female. The latter is altogether more slender and lacks the swollen hind legs. Larva feeds in dead wood. Absent from northern Europe.

3 Churchyard Beetle (*Blaps mucronata*) can be distinguished from superficially similar ground beetles (*see page 174*) by the pointed extensions at the tips of its elytra. The latter are fused together and the beetle cannot fly. It is a scavenger, usually found in and around buildings – especially damp cellars and out-houses. Larva is very like the mealworm (*page 198*), to which it is closely related.

4 *Melöe proscarabaeus* is one of the oil beetles – clumsy, flightless insects named for the smelly, oily secretions they emit when alarmed. It ranges from bluish black to purple and varies a good deal in size. Female has even smaller elytra and no kink in her antennae. Eggs are laid in the ground and young larvae crawl into flowers. They cling to solitary bees and are carried back to the nests, where they eat the eggs and then feed on the stored food. There are several similar species.

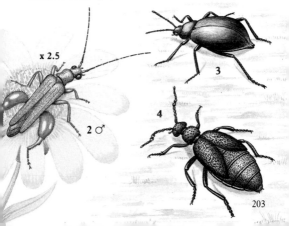

x 2.5

2 ♂

3

4

LONGHORN BEETLES

The longhorn beetles are a large group with very long antennae in most species. Males usually have longer antennae than females and also have broader tarsal segments (feet). Sizes vary a great deal within a species. Most longhorns fly well, with an undulating motion. Many are active in the sunshine, but others prefer to fly at dusk and some are strictly nocturnal. Adults nibble leaves, petals and pollen. Larvae have poorly developed legs and almost all of them feed in living or dead timber.

1 *Ergates faber* flies from twilight onwards. Female has a rougher surface to the pronotum, with less obvious tubercules in the centre. It breeds in conifer trunks and stumps in southern and central Europe. Rare in Britain.

1 ♂   2

2 Musk Beetle (*Aromia moschata*) is bright green, often with strong blue or brassy iridescence. It emits a not unpleasant musky odour. Larvae develop mainly in willows.

3 Monochamus sartor breeds in conifers, especially felled spruces, in southern and central Europe. It often does serious damage to structural timbers by continuing its depredations after the timber has been through the sawmill. The pattern of white hairs on the elytra may be less marked. It is rare in Britain – probably imported with timber.

4 House Longhorn (*Hylotrupes bajulus*) is a hairy beetle with two shiny knobs on the thorax. It breeds in dead coniferous timber and causes much damage in houses. Rare in Britain.

LONGHORN BEETLES contd.

1 *Cerambyx cerdo* is one of Europe's largest beetles. It resembles *Ergates faber* (page 204) but has a much longer head and a narrower pronotum. It flies from dusk onwards and enjoys drinking sap oozing from damaged trees. It breeds in aged oaks, especially in the evergreen oak forests of southern and central Europe. Does not live in Britain.

2 Wasp Beetle (*Clytus arietis*) is a sun-loving insect commonly seen on flowers and herbage in gardens and hedgerows. It is an excellent wasp mimic (*see Introduction*), especially when scuttling over tree trunks and waving its antennae. Larvae develop in dead deciduous timber, including fence posts and fallen branches.

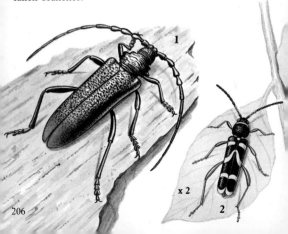

x 2

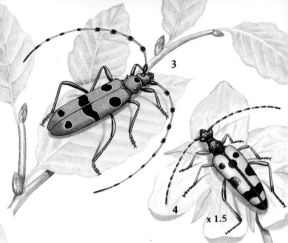

3

4

x 1.5

3 *Rosalia alpina* is a beautiful beetle with a very variable pattern of spots. It lives in upland beech-woods and breeds in the older trees. It is rare and protected by law in some countries. Does not live in Britain or northern Europe.

4 *Strangalia maculata* is most often seen on flowers and foliage in the hedgerow or woodland clearing. The elytral pattern varies, with some individuals almost entirely black, but the antennae are always yellow at the base. Larvae feed in rotting deciduous stumps. There are several similar species, all with strongly tapered elytra.

1 ×2

2 ×2

LEAF BEETLES

The leaf beetles are a very large group of vegetarians, with adults and their soft, slug-like larvae commonly sharing the same food. Some species swarm in vast numbers and may completely defoliate their food plants. Adults are often brightly coloured, some with brilliant metallic sheens, and many are smoothly rounded. Some resemble ladybirds, but they don't have clubbed antennae and they also differ in foot structure. Ladybirds have three tarsal segments, while leaf beetles have five, although only four are normally visible (*far right*).

1 *Chrysolina polita* is a very common leaf beetle displaying the typical shape and features of the group.

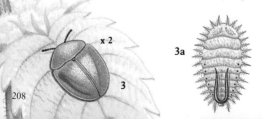

×2

3

3a

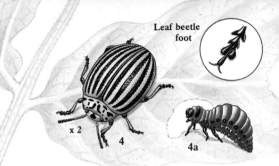

Leaf beetle foot

x 2

4

4a

It is abundant on mints and other plants in damp habitats.

2 Chrysomela populi has a black head and thorax with a very deep green sheen. The elytra are black at the very tip. Larva resembles a pale ladybird grub (*see page 201*). It feeds on sallows.

3 Cassida viridis is one of several very similar tortoise beetles. The pronotum and elytra extend beyond the edges of the body and provide excellent camouflage when the insect is resting on leaves. It feeds on mints and other labiates in damp places. Larva (**3a**) has two large spines at the rear, to which it fixes its droppings and cast skins as camouflage.

4 Colorado Beetle (*Leptinotarsa decemlineata*) and its larvae (**4a**) destroy potato plants. It also feeds on nightshades and tomato. Common on the continent, it rarely reaches Britain and must be reported to the police if found.

LEAF BEETLES contd.

1 Asparagus Beetle (*Crioceris asparagi*) is an attractive pest of asparagus. Adult hibernates and emerges as the ferny asparagus leaves are unfolding. Larvae are dirty white with black spots.

2 Bloody-nosed Beetle (*Timarcha tenebricosa*), Britain's largest leaf beetle, gets its name for its habit of exuding a drop of red fluid from its mouth when alarmed. It deters would-be predators. It is superficially similar to the dor beetle (*page 188*), but has very different legs and antennae. Flightless and slow-moving, it feeds on bedstraws and other herbs in grassy places. Larva is also black and shiny. Absent from northern Europe.

3 Turnip Flea (*Phyllotreta nemorum*) chews little holes in young seedlings of turnips and other brassicas in

x 4

1

2

x 2

spring. Larva tunnels in leaves of older plants and produces adult in autumn. The adult then hibernates. It is one of a group known as flea beetles which use their large hind legs for leaping.

4 ***Oulema melanopus*** has the head and elytra either deep blue or black, sometimes with a greenish tinge. It feeds on grasses, including cultivated cereals, and is abundant in most grassy places. It is often seen basking on sunny walls in spring.

5 ***Donacia aquatica*** can be found on waterside plants and also basking on floating leaves. Larva feeds in the submerged stems of various water plants. There are several similar species, mostly some shade of green.

x 4

3

4

x 3

5

x 2

211

WEEVILS AND BARK BEETLES

1

x 3

The weevils are a large group of beetles, mostly rather small, with the jaws at the tip of a prominent snout or rostrum. The antennae are attached to the rostrum and usually elbowed. Many weevils are decorated with colouful scales. All are vegetarians, the larvae being legless and normally feeding inside the host plant. Many feed in seeds.

1 *Curculio nucum* has one of the longest snouts, especially in the female, who uses it to bore into young hazel nuts before laying an egg in each one. Look for adults on hawthorn blooms.

2 *Phyllobius pomaceus* is one of several very similar species found on nettles throughout the summer. It is clothed with bluish green or golden green scales, but these readily rub off and older beetles generally show a good deal of black.

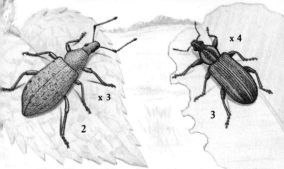

3 Pea Weevil (*Sitona lineatus*) has a broader and less prominent snout than most weevils, but its eyes are very prominent. Adults hibernate, emerging in spring to chew the leaves of peas, clovers and other legumes, producing frilly edges. Larva feeds in the root nodules.

4 Elm Bark Beetle (*Scolytus scolytus*) is the carrier of Dutch elm disease. Larvae produce characteristic patterns as they tunnel under the bark (**4a**). There are several similar species, attacking various trees and each producing its own pattern.

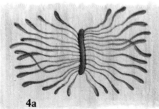

ORB-WEB SPIDERS

Spiders are not insects. They belong to the large group called arachnids (*see Introduction*). They have four pairs of legs and a body in two sections. All produce silk, although not all make webs, and all prey on insects which they paralyse with poison fangs. Females are often very much bigger than males, but males are readily recognised by their swollen palps (*see page 219*).

1 Garden Spider (*Araneus diadematus*), like the other spiders shown here, spins a more or less circular web known as an orb-web. The spiral threads are sticky

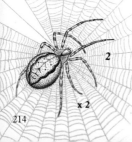

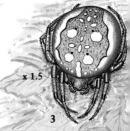

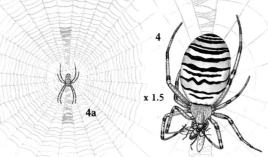

4

x 1.5

4a

and trap flying insects. Abundant in gardens and hedgerows, the spider is also known as the cross spider because of the pattern on its abdomen. Like most orb-web spiders, it passes the winter in the egg stage, safely wrapped up in little balls of silk.

2 Zygiella x-notata has a leaf-like pattern, often edged with pink, on its abdomen. Its web, usually spun across the corners of window frames and similar situations around our houses, has two empty sectors in the upper part. The spider itself generally hides in a nearby crevice.

3 Araneus quadratus is very rounded and ranges from deep green to brick-red, with four pale spots. It lives mainly on heathland shrubs.

4 Argiope bruennichi is an unmistakable spider, usually seen sitting head-down in its large web, which is slung in low-growing shrubs and other vegetation. The web has two conspicuous zig-zag bands of white silk (**4a**). Southern and central Europe.

ORB-WEB SPIDERS contd.

1 *Nuctenea umbratica* is sometimes almost entirely black and always very flat. Its web is often spun in the same places as that of *Zygiella* (*page 215*), and also on tree trunks and fences. The spider rarely emerges before dark.

2 *Tetragantha extensa* is abundant in damp vegetation, especially on river banks. The abdominal stripes range from yellow to deep orange. It makes a flimsy web without the central hub found in most orb-webs.

3 *Araniella cucurbitina* is one of our smallest orb-web spiders. The female has a greener abdomen, but both sexes have a red spot under the rear end.

4 *Cyclosa conica*, easily identified by the strange shape of its abdomen, has a variable pattern of black, brown and white and

x 3

2

1

x 2

x 3

3

x 4

4

resembles a bird dropping when sitting head-down in its web. The latter is usually spun in evergreen shrubs and generally has a band of strengthening silk as in the *Argiope* web (*page 215*).

5 *Meta segmentata* varies a good deal in colour, but can usually be recognised by the dark tuning-fork mark on the front half. It is abundant in herbaceous vegetation, usually slinging its hubless web at an angle.

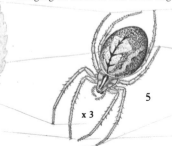

5

x 3

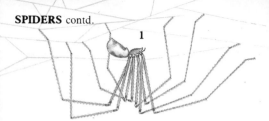

1 *Pholcus phalangioides* hangs its flimsy and irregular web in buildings. The fine threads are very hard to see. Known as the daddy-long-legs spider, it uses its long legs to throw silk over insects blundering into the web. Absent from northern Europe.

2 *Amaurobius fenestralis* makes a rather scruffy, lace-like web on damp walls and tree trunks, with the centre of the web leading to a snug retreat. Insects get their feet tangled in the thread and the spider drags them into the retreat. Similar webs on drier walls and

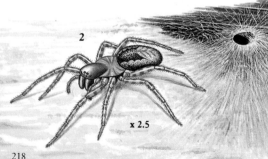

x 2.5

fences probably belong to the slightly larger *Amaurobius similis*.

3 *Linyphia triangularis* is abundant on bushes everywhere, spinning a slightly domed sheet web supported by a maze of scaffolding. The spider lurks upside-down underneath the web, waiting for insects to fall on to it after hitting the scaffolding.

4 House Spider (*Tegenaria gigantea*) is one of several similar species that run about in the house. The female is much larger than the male shown here and lacks the swollen palps. The web is a non-sticky sheet (cob-web) spun in a neglected corner.

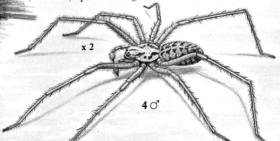

CRAB SPIDERS

The crab spiders are squat creatures with the first two pairs of legs longer than the rest. They move with a sideways shuffle, rather like some crabs. They spin no webs and ambush their prey on the ground or on vegetation. To this end, many are well camouflaged on their normal backgrounds.

1 *Xysticus cristatus* abounds in low herbage in spring and early summer, but does not lurk in flowers. The female (**1a**) is larger and paler than the male, although her coloration is variable. It feeds mainly on flies, and also takes ants. The male fixes the female to the ground, or a leaf or other surface with silken bands before mating. There are several similar species.

2 *Thomisus onustus* female is pink, yellow or white and easily identified by the large tubercules on the abdomen. Male is orange-brown and only half the female's size. They lurk in flowers. British specimens are usually pink and frequent heathers.

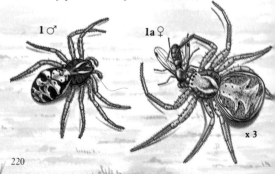

1 ♂ 1a ♀

x 3

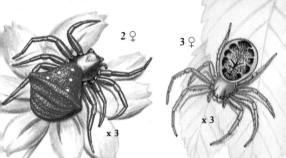

3 *Diaea dorsata*, easily identified by its colour, is usually to be found in trees and shrubs in spring and early summer. Male body is all brown.

4 *Misumena vatia* female ranges from white to pale green or yellow and can change colour slowly to match different flowers. Red stripes may be absent. It can be found – not easily – on white and yellow flowers in summer and is powerful enough to kill bees. Male is much smaller and mainly brown.

x 1.5

1

2

x 3

HUNTING SPIDERS

1 *Pisaura mirabilis* is one of the wolf spiders, chasing prey in low vegetation. Grey or brown, it can be recognised by the pale stripe on the front half, It often sunbathes, as shown, with the front two legs on each side close together. The female carries her egg cocoon in her jaws until the eggs are ready to hatch, and then fixes it to a plant and spins a silken tent over it. She stands guard until after the eggs have hatched.

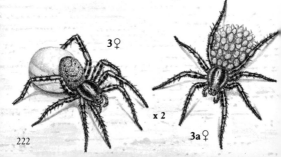

3♀

x 2

3a♀

2 Zebra Spider (*Salticus scenicus*) is one of the jumping spiders. It lives on lichen-covered rocks and walls and stalks prey until within a few centimetres. It then leaps on to it like a cat. Notice the large eyes: good sight is essential for this form of hunting.

3 *Pardosa amentata* is another wolf spider, abundant on the ground and on low vegetation everywhere. The female carries her egg cocoon attached to her spinnerets at the hind end, and the youngsters ride on her back for a few days after hatching (**3a**). There are several very similar species.

4 *Dolomedes fimbriatus* lives at the edges of ponds and also in swamps and marshes with patches of open water, often basking on floating leaves. The female is less boldly marked than the male and about twice his size. She also lacks the swollen palps typical of all male spiders. Prey includes all kinds of insects and even small fishes.

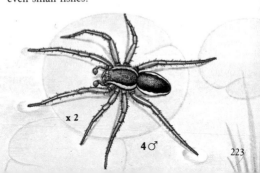

x 2

4♂

HUNTING SPIDERS contd.

1 *Drassodes lapidosus* hides in a silken chamber under logs and stones by day and emerges to hunt at night. It is a powerful creature whose prey includes other large spiders as well as insects. It commonly lurks in the garden shed.

2 *Dysdera crocata* is another nocturnal hunter, specialising in woodlice, which it grabs and pierces with its enormous jaws. It spends the day in a silken chamber under a log or stone. Absent from northern Europe.

3 *Zelotes apricorum* is closely related to *Drassodes* and has similar habits. The nipple-shaped pink egg cocoon (**3a**) characteristic of this large genus is

x 2

1

2

x 2

produced in the female's retreat. There are several similar species, differing in the amount of brown on the legs.

4 Scytodes thoracica is an unmistakable spider in which the two parts of the body are more or less equal. Normally found only in houses, although it may occur out of doors in southern Europe, it is active mainly by night. It is commonly called the spitting spider, because of its unique method of catching food. It stalks its prey slowly – usually concentrating on small flies – and when within about 6mm it fires two strands of quick-setting gum from its jaws. At the same time it vibrates its jaws rapidly from side to side and the victim is pinned to the surface with two zig-zag threads. The spider can then feed at its leisure. The gum reservoirs are in the front half of the body.

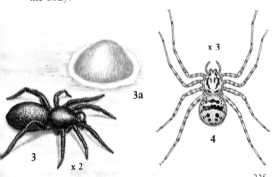

3a

3

x 2

x 3

4

SCORPIONS and HARVESTMEN

Scorpions are nocturnal arachnids, catching various insects and other prey with their pincers. The sting at the tip of the tail is mainly for defence.

1 *Euscorpius flavicaudis* is the commonest of the few European species. Harmless to us, it inhabits crevices in rocks and old walls and grabs passing prey. It is a native of southern Europe, but a few small colonies are established in Britain.

Harvestmen differ from spiders in the single body unit with just two eyes on a turret on the top. The animals are basically scavengers, with no venom and no silk. Most species mature in autumn.

2 *Phalangium opilio* is pure white underneath. Female lacks horns on her jaws. It is abundant in dense vegetation and active mainly at night.

3 *Leiobunum rotundum* is common on walls and vegetation. Female has a longer and more oval body.

4 *Megabunus diadema*, with a bristly eye-turret, matures in spring and is found on tree trunks.

x 2

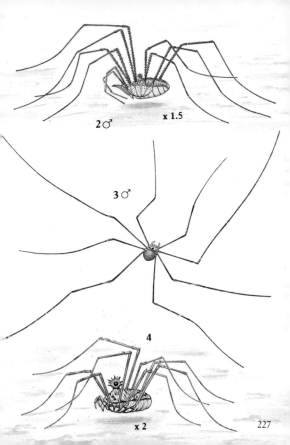

2♂   x 1.5

3♂

4

x 2

CENTIPEDES

Centipedes belong to the group of arthropods known as chilopods. Although centipede literally means 100 feet, no species has precisely that number. There is one pair to each body segment, and our British centipedes bear from 15 to 101 pairs when mature. The last pair are usually longer than the rest and act like an extra pair of antennae. Centipedes are all predatory creatures with poison fangs curving around the head. They usually hide by day and hunt by night for a wide range of other animals – including other centipedes. Most are harmless to us, but a few southern European species can deliver a painful bite.

1 Scutigera coleoptrata has 15 pairs of legs and runs extremely fast. It often lives in buildings but occurs only sporadically in Britain – probably brought in with produce from southern Europe.

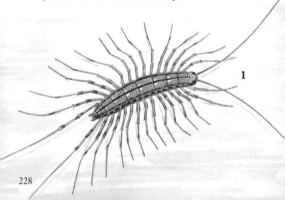

1

2 *Cryptops hortensis* has 21 pairs of legs, with the last pair particularly stout. It lives under logs and stones in woods and gardens.

3 *Necrophloeophagus longicornis* is one of the soil-living centipedes that you commonly turn up in your garden. Often wrongly called the wireworm, it has 49 or 51 pairs of legs.

4 *Lithobius forficatus* can be found under logs and stones almost everywhere. It has 15 pairs of legs when mature, but only 7 pairs when a baby. There are several similar species.

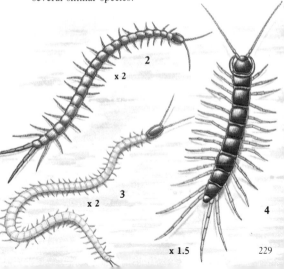

2

x 2

x 2

3

4

x 1.5

MILLIPEDES

The millipedes belong to the group of arthropods known as diplopods, a name based on the fact that each body segment has two pairs of legs. This feature readily distinguishes them from the centipedes (*page 228*). The English name means 1000 feet, but no European species approaches this number. Millipedes are vegetarians, feeding mainly on decaying material, although they will nibble tender growing plants. They are generally active at night, but some come out after daytime rains. Many produce foul-smelling secretions from glands all along the sides of the body, but not all their enemies are deterred by this: toads and starlings eat lots of millipedes.

1 Pill Millipede (*Glomeris marginata*) differs from the pill woodlouse (*page 233*) in having more legs and in its shinier and blacker coat. It is one of several similar species, all able to roll into a ball (**1a**). Some

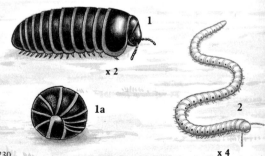

1

x 2

1a

2

x 4

continental species are decorated with red stripes and spots. They all live mainly in grassy places.

2 Spotted Snake Millipede (*Blaniulus guttulatus*) lives in the soil and may damage potatoes and other crops. The red spots are the repellent glands.

3 *Polydesmus angustus* is one of the flat-backed millipedes. Each segment is basically cylindrical, but has a flange on each side to produce the flat appearance. With 20 body segments, it lives mainly in leaf litter and is common in the compost heap.

4 *Cylindroiulus londinensis* is one of several very similar species coiling into a spiral when disturbed. It has about 46 body segments and, unlike several of its close relatives, it is more or less the same thickness throughout. It lives in decaying vegetation and can often be found under logs and loose bark.

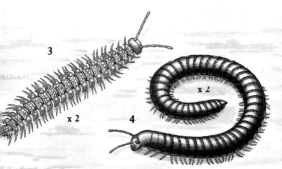

3

x 2

x 2

4

WOODLICE

The woodlice are land-living crustaceans, more closely related to crabs than to the insects and other arthropods described earlier in this book. They still require a fairly moist environment, however, and venture forth only at night to browse on decaying vegetation and on algae growing on walls and tree trunks. They sometimes nibble young seedlings, especially in greenhouses. All have seven pairs of walking legs, largely concealed under the broad plates of the thorax or pereion. The hind part of the body is the pleon and carries a pair of forked limbs called uropods at the rear which are probably sensory and also exude a repellent secretion to ward off predators.

1 *Oniscus asellus* is abundant under logs and in the compost heap. The flagellum of the antenna – beyond the longest segment – has three segments.

2 *Porcellio scaber* is another very common species, tolerating drier places than *Oniscus* and often found

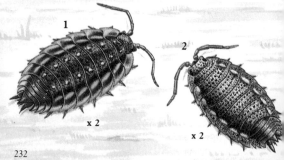

x 2

x 2

on walls and tree trunks. Much less shiny than *Oniscus*, it has only two flagellar segments.

3 Pill-bug (*Armadillidium vulgare*) can live in even drier places than *Porcellio*. Its ability to roll into a ball helps it to conserve moisture. The greyish coat and the numerous small segments at the rear help to distinguish it from the pill millipede (*page 230*) when rolled up (**3a**). It lives mainly in grassy places.

4 *Armadillidium maculatum* is a close relative of the last species, found under stones in dry grassland. It is confined to southern France and neighbouring parts of Italy.

5 *Philoscia muscorum* has a sharp division between pereion and pleon instead of the smooth transition seen in the other species. It ranges from yellowish to deep brown, always with a dark stripe along the back. It is especially common in damp grassland.

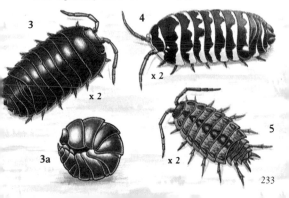

3

4

x 2

3a

x 2

5

x 2

Index